WORTH
DYING FOR

A NAVY SEAL'S CALL TO A NATION

RORKE DENVER
AND ELLIS HENICAN

HOWARD BOOKS
AN IMPRINT OF SIMON & SCHUSTER, INC.

NEW YORK   NASHVILLE   LONDON   TORONTO   SYDNEY   NEW DELHI

Howard Books
An Imprint of Simon & Schuster, Inc.
1230 Avenue of the Americas
New York, NY 10020

First Howard Books trade paperback edition January 2017

HOWARD and colophon are trademarks of Simon & Schuster, Inc.

For information about special discounts for bulk purchases, please contact Simon & Schuster Special Sales at 1-866-506-1949 or business@simonandschuster.com.

The Simon & Schuster Speakers Bureau can bring authors to your live event. For more information or to book an event, contact the Simon & Schuster Speakers Bureau at 1-866-248-3049 or visit our website at www.simonspeakers.com.

Manufactured in the United States of America

10   9   8   7   6   5   4   3   2   1

The Library of Congress has cataloged the hardcover edition as:

Names: Denver, Rorke, author. | Henican, Ellis author.
Title: Worth dying for : a Navy SEAL's call to a nation / Rorke Denver and Ellis Henican.
Description: First Howard Books hardcover edition. | New York : Howard Books, 2016.
Identifiers: LCCN 2015034024
Subjects: LCSH: United States. Navy. SEALs. | United States. Navy—Commando troops. | War on Terrorism, 2001–2009. | Terrorism—Prevention. | Denver, Rorke.
Classification: LCC VG87 .D45 2016 | DDC 359.9/84—dc23 LC record available at http://lccn.loc.gov/2015034024

ISBN 978-1-5011-2411-2
ISBN 978-1-5011-2568-3 (pbk)
ISBN 978-1-5011-2413-6 (ebook)

For all those who have chosen to serve—in a thousand different ways

CONTENTS

INTRODUCTION

A nation that draws too broad a difference between its scholars and its warriors will have its thinking done by cowards and its fighting done by fools.
—THUCYDIDES (460–400 BC)

A ncient Greece had nothing on modern America.

As I look around our nation today, the words of Thucydides keep bouncing inside my head. I see divisions at least as troubling as the ones the Greek general and historian warned about nearly twenty-five hundred years ago. On the civilian side, there's a disturbing disconnect from the military. It's not just that fewer Americans serve now. It's that many people don't even know anyone who does. On the military side, there's a deepening mistrust of civilian leadership and an increasing frustration at being misunderstood. American soldiers and American civilians still pledge allegiance to the same stars and stripes. But how can we ever hope to understand each other if we live like two separate tribes?

The civilians say, "You take care of all the messy stuff." The soldiers say, "Then let us do our jobs."

But I am a thinker *and* a fighter. I am an engaged U.S. citizen and a fiercely loyal U.S. Navy SEAL. A bridge builder by temperament and a warrior by trade, I believe that despite our many differences, most Americans really are on the same side. We love our country. We want what's best for it. We have strong feelings about what that might entail, even when we keep those feelings to ourselves or share them only with a few like-minded relatives and friends. Until recently, people in our country weren't content to leave the politics to the politicians, the professing to the professors, or the soldiering to the men and women in uniform. Why start now?

One of the most powerful forces our Founding Fathers set loose nearly two and a half centuries ago was the idea of everyday citizens energetically engaged in defining a future that belonged to everyone and then helping to make it real. We need to ignite that spirit of patriotic service again. With this book, I hope to light that fuse.

I have been training for this duty as long as I can recall. A lifelong patriot, a Division I athlete, a voracious reader, a multidisciplinary scholar, a veteran officer in a premier U.S. special-operations fighting force. I had thirteen years of very active SEAL duty: deployed to Central and South America, East and West Africa, Afghanistan and Iraq. Leading two hundred successful combat missions. Helping to create Iraq's Sunni awakening in 2006. Running every phase of SEAL training, from day-one induction to Hell Week to our advanced finishing schools. Advising a senior SEAL admiral on a wide range of issues from deck-plate discipline to matters of deep national concern. Briefing congressional committees on special-operations readiness. On Navy orders, I represented the SEAL brotherhood by taking a leading role in the real-life action-adventure film *Act of Valor*. We made sure our story was told authentically and compellingly enough to create a number one Hollywood blockbuster that the teams could also feel was speaking for them. My first book, *Damn Few*, was a multiweek *New York Times* best seller that explained how the SEALs are creating a new generation of warriors uniquely suited for the asymmetrical threats America faces today. Now I'm a successful public speaker and leadership consultant, advising top companies on teamwork, motivation, and high-performance techniques. Helping people work together is what I have always done, in military and civilian life.

As a Navy SEAL officer at war, a key part of my duty was to create common ground among a team of talented but headstrong individuals. At the start of any new mission,

I liked to pull fifteen to twenty adrenaline-fueled special operators into a room—snipers, breachers, communicators, translators, and the rest. All of them would be itching for action, coiled and ready to strike. They all had strong notions about how to accomplish the next assault. I would arrive with a clear plan in my own mind. But however many guys there were in the briefing room, that's how many opinions we had. I'd listen carefully to my men. I'd give everyone a chance to contribute and be heard. I'd encourage them to weigh one another's ideas. With all of their input and my own insights, I'd forge a battle plan that everyone would be expected to get behind. That was my job—to build that plan and to rally those troops. Then we'd go out and get lethal, assaulting a target or barreling around the IEDs on a pockmarked highway or walking a foot patrol through an urban-enemy sniper nest, risking our lives together as a well-oiled, singularly focused, action-ready team. It's a fascinating process—bringing that team together—and a beautiful thing to behold.

Contrast that with the way America now confronts its largest issues. Pundits are shouting. Washington is paralyzed. Prejudices are festering. Motives are questioned. Blue states are certain that red states are heartless. Red states are certain that blue states are clueless. There's little core agreement on what makes America great. And the world gets dicier every day. With each new issue that comes spinning around, too many people pick a side, hold on tight, and choose not to be bothered with other points of view. This may sound hopeless, but it doesn't have to be. SEALs always have a plan.

America asks a lot of its warriors, expecting us to carry the weight of the nation solidly on our shoulders. The SEALs ask even more. Every day, we are expected to "earn the Trident"—that's the expression we use. The Trident is our warfare insignia. On the rare occasions a SEAL wears his uniform, you'll see a golden Trident pin above the other medals and decorations on the left side of his chest. Look closely. There's a lot of meaning in that symbol. The spear is a nod to Poseidon and our maritime heritage. The old flintlock pistol is cocked and ready like SEALs are expected to be. The American eagle has its head bowed, reminding us to remain humble at all times. Every branch of the service has its own symbolic guideposts. The Trident is ours. But all of us in uniform, regardless of where we serve, advance hugely complex interests in horribly confusing parts of the world. We are sent into battle with inadequate numbers on missions frequently ill-defined. The allies are iffy. The cultures are damn near impenetrable. The enemies are deeply entrenched. And we keep performing brilliantly. When the mission takes too long or spills too much blood, the public quickly turns impatient.

The veterans are welcomed home with slapdash support and a few kind words. "Thank you for your service," though appreciated, goes only so far.

Upon our return, hardly anyone asks us what we have learned or how we might contribute, least of all the leaders who sent us off to war. What have we discovered about our enemies? Where are the fault lines in this clash of cultures? Which wars can be brought to satisfying conclusions and which ones cannot? What do our troops need most as they get on with their lives? Warriors know things that politicians don't have a clue about. These warriors have to be pulled into the national dialogue.

The pundits have spoken. The policy makers have too. So have the politicians and interest groups. Warriors are rarely the first to the microphone or the keyboard. We usually deliver our messages by other, more violent means. But fifteen years into our latest conflicts, it's long past time for a fresh, terror-age take on what it is we are fighting and sometimes dying for and what lessons we have learned along the way.

As a special-operations military professional, I refuse to be a captive of any particular political ideology or social outlook. In my experience, they all have severe limitations—though also make some valuable contributions. The best people in uniform are experts at achieving impossible tasks in highly challenging environments—keeping the goal clearly in mind, whatever the threats and limitations may be. SEALs are better at this than anyone else. We've been out there, doing the nation's business. We and America's other thoughtful warriors should be heard.

Like many thinking warriors, I take guidance from important strategists and leaders who have come before me. Thucydides isn't the only one. There's Sun Tzu, Clausewitz, Lincoln, Churchill—I can't begin to imagine how much poorer my thinking would be if it weren't for their fertile minds.

As I wrestle with these issues, it is Marcus Aurelius who provided the structure of how to proceed. The Roman emperor from AD 161 to 180 left a collection of private notes to himself, twelve books in all, that together are known as his *Meditations*. He did not intend for them to be published. They were for his own self-improvement. Together, they provide a unique and candid view of a great leader's thinking as he plans a series of bold military campaigns. His writing style is unpretentious. He has a stoic attitude and a strong ethical sense. Even two thousand years later, you get a vivid sense of a brilliant mind at work.

"Waste no more time arguing about what a good man should be," he writes. "Be one."

"Dwell on the beauty of life. Watch the stars, and see yourself running with them."

"Never let the future disturb you. You will meet it, if you have to, with the same weapons of reason which today arm you against the present."

"If someone is able to show me that what I think or do is not right, I will happily change, for I seek the truth, by which no one was ever truly harmed. It is the person who continues in his self-deception and ignorance who is harmed."

It is stunning to know that he wrote all of this two millennia ago.

I take his words not only as inspiration but also as a challenge. Our experiences at war, his and mine, were very different but also parallel in many ways. His station in life was far more elevated than mine will ever be, but he sets an excellent standard of inquiry.

In the pages to come, I will apply my officer's insights and battlefield experience—my own unique SEAL-sense—to ten pressing issues raised by America's new era at war. What makes a hero. How to be brave. The right and the wrong ways to kill. How we can better align military and civilian America. What we really owe our returning veterans. There will be a lot of talk about service, which is where everything else begins. My aim here isn't to cover every aspect of being a warrior for America or a nation semipermanently at war. Instead, I will focus on a handful of key topics and lay down some broader principles. I want to help create a common language for a smarter public conversation, despite our dumbed-down politics and a gaping military-civilian divide.

Let's reconnect our soldiers and our scholars and everyday Americans too. Everyone needs to be in this fight. We can't afford to leave the country we love in the dangerous hands of cowards and fools.

CHAPTER 1

SEND ME A HERO

Not long ago, I was the guest speaker at a middle school in Texas. The teachers and students couldn't have been more welcoming—when I walked into the auditorium, half a dozen American flags were lined up on the stage. The entire school, it seemed, had come to hear me. The school's principal, a friendly man in a plaid sport coat, announced that "a real war hero has come to share his experiences with us today." I couldn't help myself. When he said that, I glanced over my shoulder to get a look at this hero he was referring to.

Our culture craves heroes. Often I hear people say, "There aren't enough heroes anymore," and I understand the sentiment. We all need someone to admire. Someone to measure ourselves against. Someone who exhibits qualities the rest of us can emulate. It certainly feels to me like we could all use a few more of those. But *heroic* isn't how I see myself or how my SEAL teammates see themselves. To us, applying that word to ourselves is almost like claiming an undeserved prize. It might look shiny at first, but it's hard to imagine ever really enjoying it. In the minds of most warriors, the heroes are the ones who didn't make it home, the ones who gave that last, full measure of themselves and never returned from the battlefield. Those are the people we hold in our hearts as heroes. The rest of us are just doing our jobs.

SEALs never use the word *heroic* as we head out on a mission. We're much too focused on the last-minute, practical things. "Are the trucks fueled up?" "Do we have a solid navigation plan?" "Have we built in the right contingencies?" If anything, I have wondered, "Will today be the day that my bravery is tested profoundly?" knowing I can never predict what might arrive or when.

I'm not reaching for false humility here. Most of the time, war is just dirty, ugly work. The day-to-day stuff is straight labor—dangerous labor, maybe, but labor nonetheless. Prepping our gear. Loading the vehicles. Getting from here to there. Stopping to kick in a door, set up an ambush, or find suitable terrain for a fight. I wouldn't call it heroic. I wouldn't even call it brave. I would call it a tough and important job that in certain, rare moments can lead toward heroism or be deemed heroic by others. But mostly, we get in. We get it done. We get out—all of us, if we've done our jobs effectively—alive. Day in and day out, that's what war is.

I have won awards including a high-ranking one, the Bronze Star with "V" for valorous action in combat. I appreciated the honor, but when someone looks at me, or someone else in the military, and uses that heavyweight word, it feels awkward. My first reaction is almost always the one I had in that middle school auditorium, some version of "There must be someone in the room with shinier medals or who has lived a more exemplary life than I have."

When good people say, "Thank you for your service," I understand it comes from a place of appreciation and respect. So "thank you" is what I told that principal as I launched into my talk that day—and left it at that.

With that simple, polite exchange, I was reminded that we are stuck with outmoded archetypes of who even qualifies to be called a hero. It's easy to say the hero is the guy who hit the home run in the ninth inning to win the World Series or did something dramatic on the battlefield that won him a Silver Star. Yes, every first responder at 9/11 can be called a hero for passing the personal-sacrifice test, running toward the dust and tragedy of the collapsing towers to help those in need. All these acts are good and deserving of our praise. But so is whispering just the right words into the ear of a child at exactly the right moment. We need to be more discerning and broaden our understanding of what a hero is. Hardly anyone ever calls a mailman, truck driver, schoolteacher, or stay-at-home mom a hero. Maybe we should. Without a doubt, some of them deserve it.

There is something terribly out of whack today about the way we pick our heroes. We get fixated on high-profile stars, athletes, and people who work in a handful of supposedly heroic professions—soldiers and police officers, firefighters and trauma surgeons—and we pretty much leave it at that. In truth, athletes worth emulating are few and far between. Heroic billionaires and business tycoons are certainly rare. Actors play heroes, but how many of today's celebrities truly behave heroically? Who among the current crop of stars has dropped out of that glitzy lifestyle to go serve—and I don't just mean militarily. Which one of them has sacrificed anything? As far as I can tell, almost all of their charitable works are accompanied by press releases and paparazzi photo ops. There was once an era when athletes and the Hollywood elite actually said, "I'm going to pick up a gun in one of the world wars," or "I'm putting my film career on hold and returning to Ohio to care for my aged mother." It's been a while.

After years of thinking about this, I have come to understand that heroism lives in many forms and in many different kinds of people. It extends beyond dying on the battlefield, the definition my teammates and I find reflexive refuge in. Nor can the concept of what constitutes a hero be limited to the familiar categories. I live in one of those categories, and I can tell you without a shadow of a doubt that the pool of potential heroes is a whole lot deeper than the people who are running back an interception for a touchdown or walking a red carpet or killing a bunch of bad guys in a war zone. *Dead* can't be the only defining characteristic of heroism. Nor can fame. Nor can money. Nor can the number of Facebook followers someone has.

We need to step back for a minute and think this through. What exactly is a hero? What is it that makes someone's service, someone's sacrifice, someone's bravery, stand out heroically? Most people don't have a clue where to start looking, much less an understanding of what really makes a hero. I've had the privilege to know many true heroes—people who served their country in the military—and people who didn't. While those who deserve to be called "hero" don't all possess the same precise mix of traits, my experience has taught me that true heroes do share a few core characteristics in common. Let me tell you what I think they are.

HEROES PUT OTHERS FIRST

Personal sacrifice is at the very heart of heroism, a willingness to put the needs of others first, even at extraordinary personal cost. That's why Pat Tillman stood out for so many. A future superstar in the NFL, he had always exceeded his potential. He wasn't physically big enough to play football, and yet he played spectacularly. He had a huge career ahead of him when he did something remarkable. In 2002, eight months after 9/11 and four days after Memorial Day, he left his promising life as an NFL player to join the Army Rangers. He went to Afghanistan and was tragically killed in action. For someone like Pat, just being there—when he had so many reasons not to be—was heroic.

Malala Yousafzai was this kind of hero. I've never met her, though I'd like to one day. Malala was born in Pakistan into a family that believed deeply in education—for girls as well as boys. When she was old enough, she began attending a school her father had founded just as the strict Taliban government had begun tightening its brutal grip on Pakistan. The Taliban staunchly opposed the education of girls.

Malala could have said nothing and continued her schooling in secret at her father's school. But remaining silent would not have helped her classmates and the many thousands of other girls who wanted to learn but didn't have access to education.

At age eleven, Malala took up their cause in a risky and public way. She gave a speech entitled "How Dare the Taliban Take Away My Basic Right to Education." Four months later, Malala started blogging for the BBC about the Taliban's efforts to prohibit females from obtaining education. Three years after her first speech, she was nominated for the International Children's Peace Prize. The Taliban's response: issue a death threat against Malala.

When she was fourteen, a man with a gun boarded her school bus and demanded to know which of the students was Malala. Glances in Malala's direction gave her away. The man fired, shooting her in the side of her head. After being flown to England to undergo multiple operations, she recovered from her injuries and refused to be silent. She continued to speak out on behalf of universal education, even taking her cause to the United Nations in New York.

She's one tough young woman and an inspiration to me, as brave as anyone I have ever known or heard about. Standing defiantly for the rights of others, suffering the consequences, and still pressing on—clearly she is someone worth emulating and looking up to. She absolutely deserved the Nobel Peace Prize she won at age seventeen, and I don't believe she's remotely done.

Without ever picking up a gun, Malala is fighting the same enemies those of us in the military have been fighting, the same force of darkness and oppression in the same part of the world. And frankly, she's been able to achieve results that far exceed what we've done with all our weapons and tactics. That's undeniably heroic.

HEROES DO THE RIGHT THINGS FOR THE RIGHT REASONS

To me, the people who most deserve to be called heroes are everyday folks who do everyday things extraordinarily well. I make this point when I talk to youth groups and to corporate audiences. Consider the schoolteacher who uses her own money to buy supplies for her classroom. She doesn't do it to end up on the front page of a magazine or the star of a YouTube video. What about the nurse who stays a few minutes after her shift is over to spend time with an elderly patient who has no family. These everyday heroes don't receive a lot of praise for what they do, but they get the job done. Simple acts can qualify as heroism. I see it happen every day.

My parents split when I was young. My mom was a single mother living in the Silicon Valley of Northern California in a very expensive part of the world—maxing out credit cards, doing whatever was necessary to provide for my brother and me. This was no small feat. Still, we were able to take awesome trips. While my friends were flying off to Europe with their families on spring vacation, my mom, my brother, and I were driving across America in a beat-up Subaru. My mom always found a way, making her someone I consider a hero. Whatever realm they're operating in, that's what a certain kind of hero does. Facing the mundane difficulties of day-to-day life, they just keep going.

Of course, we love it when our heroes dazzle us. After all, we look to them to inspire us toward greatness. Chesley Sullenberger certainly did that. The celebrated US Airways captain landed a disabled Airbus A320 on the Hudson River, saving all 155 people aboard. Sully's perfect water landing soon after takeoff from LaGuardia Airport took him from private to public hero in a matter of seconds, though I have the impression he is still very much the same man he always was.

But it wasn't just Sully's training or calm under pressure that made him a hero. It wasn't even his awe-inspiring competence. What made him a hero was that he did his job superbly, and he didn't view that as anything extraordinary. He was just discharging the obligation he undertook when he climbed into the cockpit of a commercial jetliner with passengers aboard. After he performed his job that day, he didn't go around patting himself on the back for the next six months. Sully didn't feel a need to be on the front of a cereal box or star in a reality TV show.

Cal Ripkin Jr. was loaded with talent. A beloved infielder with the Baltimore Orioles, his stats included 3,184 hits, 431 home runs, and 1,695 runs batted in. He won two Golden Glove Awards, made the American League All-Star Team nineteen times, and was the league's Most Valuable Player twice. But that isn't what made Cal a hero to me or to most real baseball fans. There are a lot of talented ballplayers out there, but talent isn't the same as character. It was the oddball film director Woody Allen who once famously declared, "Eighty percent of success is showing up." Cal Ripkin Jr. showed up. He showed up no matter what. He played in an astounding 2,632 games in a row, never once calling in sick, injured, or too hungover to play. In twenty-one seasons with the Orioles, the Hall of Fame infielder became one of the most productive players in baseball history. He broke Lou Gehrig's fifty-six-year-old record for consecutive games played. He behaved like a grown-up in a game of overgrown boys. Heroism is meeting your responsibilities, big or small, not for praise or money, but because it's the right thing to do.

HEROES SEE THE WORLD AS IT SHOULD BE

Heroes see beyond the place they are. Winston Churchill embodied this kind of hero, the visionary. He presciently saw the world around him. Well in advance of World War II, he predicted the growing evil in Germany that would have to be dealt with. Skillfully, he played the puzzle pieces on the board as he calculated how to get the American president, Franklin Delano Roosevelt, into the fight and how he could make waves before Pearl Harbor was ever bombed. Churchill foresaw all of this. Not only that, he also understood before almost anyone else that an Iron Curtain was descending and the Soviet Union would be the next real problem. His understanding of the world was staggering—allowing him to make the heroic decisions that were necessary.

Our Founding Fathers were heroes because of their vision of what this country could be as much as for their prowess on the battlefield. Washington, Madison, Jefferson, Hamilton, Franklin: think of how much these men achieved in their lives and how much effort they expended getting there. I like my heroes to be dogged and determined as they achieve great things. Working, studying, thinking, strategizing—when did they ever have time to rest? They were inventors, philosophers, and statesmen and, by the way, they also managed to create a brand-new country that became the greatest country on earth. Ben Franklin wasn't sitting around tweeting on social media for attention, I promise you that. He never got tired of improving the world around him. He was in his study or workshop, solving problems, designing things, and asking himself deep, philosophical questions. The full extent of what he and the others gave our country is mind-boggling.

The men who founded this country imagined a better way for people to govern themselves. And they put themselves on the line to achieve that vision. They said, in effect: "We pledge our lives, our fortunes, and our sacred honor to this vital cause." I ask, who today is willing to commit so much now? These heroes did it, fully recognizing the risks involved and with incredible vision of America's future.

HEROES ARE TOUGH ENOUGH TO SHOW HUMILITY

I take regular muster of my heroes, an exercise I would highly recommend everyone do. I reflect on what makes these people heroes to me, beyond a willingness to risk their lives. I ask myself: What characteristics do I most admire? Who has them in abundance? Whose life inspires mine?

My brother, Nate, always comes to mind. He is smart, creative, skilled, physically aggressive, tough, fit, and hard.

Nate's a firefighter in Los Angeles, which is a high-pressure, high-risk, high-energy calling. And firefighters in L.A. do a lot more than fight fires; they are in the lifesaving business, responding to human emergencies of every imaginable sort. Nate doesn't brag, but if you ask him, he'll tell you harrowing stories about mangled bodies he's pulled from auto freeway accidents, flatlined cardiac patients he's brought back to life, and many people he's helped who were simply going through life when suddenly some great calamity befell them. In those moments, Nate can't wait to get into the action.

Three years my junior, he's monkey-gorilla strong and ambitious. He bought a house and fixed it up on his own. He'd never been trained to do this, but he did it exquisitely. He has a beautiful handmade wooden table in his living room. I came inside one day and asked, "Man, where did you get that table?"

"I built it," he said simply.

That's just Nate.

"I just fought a three-alarm fire . . . I pulled someone out of a burning car . . . I benched three hundred and ten pounds . . . I built an exquisite table with my own hands." Most people would be posting daily photos and weekly progress reports. Not Nate. He's done all those things and barely mentions them in conversation. It's just what he does and who he is.

John McCain, a true war hero, exemplifies humility under duress. When Donald Trump was campaigning to be the 2016 Republican nominee for president, the real-estate mogul and reality TV star made light of Senator John McCain's five years as a prisoner of war in North Vietnam. "He was a war hero because he was captured?" Trump scoffed during an appearance at the Family Leadership Summit in Ames, Iowa. "I like people who weren't captured."

Veterans around the country erupted in outrage, but the former naval aviator McCain kept his cool. He didn't demand that Trump apologize to him. "I think he may owe an apology to the families of those who have sacrificed in conflict and those who have undergone the prison experience of serving their country," McCain said.

Then McCain said something interesting about heroism, something I could certainly hear a SEAL say. "I'm not a hero," he went on, "but those who were my senior ranking officers, people like Colonel Bud Day, a Congressional Medal of Honor winner, and those that have inspired us to do things that we otherwise wouldn't have been capable of doing. Those are the people that I think he owes an apology to."

McCain knew. Heroes don't grab credit, even when there are political points to score. They don't take personal insult. They rise above the dumb and the trivial. And that's part of what inspires the rest of us to be better than we are.

THE CARE HEROES DESERVE

This hero business carries heavy burdens. Many of our heroes are imperfect people, once you get to know them, or their heroism is limited to just one part of their lives. Churchill drank too much. Some of the Founding Fathers owned slaves. Often, heroism is something that occurs during one extraordinary season, one unimaginable tour of duty, one single moment of action. Then it's back to regular life. That can be a tough adjustment. There's a reason many high school sports stars have tough middle-aged lives. There's also an explanation why many great warriors retell tales of their glory days for the next fifty years.

Heroes, people who have achieved phenomenally, often face difficulties when their moment of glory is done. Suddenly they are regular people again. And yet, as officially declared heroes, they are held to the wildly elevated standards of heroism. It's an uncomfortable situation to be in, often a huge psychological burden.

As a friend put it to me: "What I did turned into a heroic moment. Now I'm just trying to pay my cable bill and be a good father, brother, or son, and I might fail. It's a heavy expectation even if people really don't know what they're throwing on your shoulders." Going back to an ordinary life after war is a tough adjustment.

I have another friend—an undeniable war hero—who said to me: "I don't know what I'm supposed to be now. I didn't announce, 'I'm a hero.' I just happened to be in a place where three hundred bad guys charged my buddies, and I survived. If that same event happens again, there is no reason to think I'll be the one telling the tale. Yet people expect so much from me. I'm not sure that's who I am."

Many warriors I know who have won prestigious awards and survived dangerous events have found themselves saying, "Damn, did I get lucky! What now?"

Those are the voices of real-life heroes. These people carry the label, but they still aren't always sure it applies to them.

These heroes try to compartmentalize. They go back to their jobs and don't discuss their war experiences. Or they say as little as possible: "I was a Marine . . . I did what they asked me to . . . I was lucky to get home alive."

It's their way of lowering expectations, cutting short the dicey conversations, and easing more gently into civilian life. It's a survival mechanism, and it is fully their right to say, "Now I'm back in Oklahoma, and I'm going to go back to the farm." War heroes are just as likely to be humble, even uncertain of their own heroism. Most, I have found, would be very happy to avoid any limelight at all.

The returning war veteran, the retired sports star, the fire-fighter whose firefighting days are done—hardly anyone is a hero always and everywhere. That's an awful lot to ask. We are free to pick and choose the characteristics in individuals we admire and try to learn from—and sometimes even ignore things that some might say detract from the good. We are inspired by their bravery and achievements. We seek to emulate the extraordinary things they have done. We are reminded by their selfless choices of the values that we ourselves try to hold. But they are not cartoon superheroes; they are complex people trying to get by.

Don't forget this. We owe our heroes space. The space to be themselves. The space not to be heroes every day. The space, outside of their heroism, to live real lives. In return, we get inspiration—not perfection—from them. We should be grateful when we get that much.

FINDING YOUR INNER HERO

Many heroes never consciously prepare themselves for the acts that define them as heroes. Whatever their special fuel was—boldness, selflessness, religious faith, personal bravery—it must have been present inside them already. Like a shooting star in the darkness, it seemed to ignite almost on its own. But this doesn't mean heroism doesn't reside within all of us. On August 21, 2015, three young vacationing

Americans—Spencer Stone, Alek Skarlatos, and Anthony Sadler—were on a high-speed train from Paris to Amsterdam. Five hundred and fifty-one other passengers were also aboard that day. Outside Brussels, a twenty-five-year-old Moroccan terrorist stepped out of a restroom armed with an AKM assault rifle, a 9mm Luger pistol, a box cutter, and a bottle of gasoline. There was no time to think or make a plan or call for help. All three Americans jumped up to tackle the man. Spencer Stone, who serves in the U.S. Air Force, later said, "You can't live your life in a cocoon or in fear. You have to act when you need to act. I thought when I ran toward him, I would be mowed down before I got to him—but maybe Alek could get to him or Anthony."

He acted anyway. Heroes act anyway.

"When I heard the click of the gun to the back of my head, I thought this is it," Stone said. But the gun didn't fire. "I thought when he slashed me with the box cutter, he would slice my artery. But none of that happened. God was there with us."

These three young friends foiled that attack not because of what they knew or how they planned. They foiled the attack because they had heroism inside them.

Truly, in this hair-trigger world of ours, there are endless opportunities for heroism. Three months after the attempted train attack, on November 13, 2015, terrorists struck successfully in Paris, killing 130 people and injuring another 368. Sadly, no one had a chance to overwhelm the perpetrators, but there were heroes nonetheless. They were the ones who rushed in without concern for their own safety and provided medical care. In one memorable case, these heroes rescued a pregnant woman who was left hanging on the side of a building trying to escape the carnage. Again, the heroes acted not just because of what they saw. They acted because of who they are. Across our long history, such heroes turn up everywhere.

Joshua Chamberlain understood what it means to be a hero. He was a professor at Bowdoin College in Maine with no military training of any sort, who volunteered to fight with the Union Army in the Civil War. Though he had never studied military strategy, he rose to the rank of brigadier general and earned a Medal of Honor for extraordinary personal bravery at Gettysburg. So beloved was he by his men, he was given the honor of commanding the Union troops at Robert E. Lee's surrender at the Appomattox Court House in Virginia. After the war, Chamberlain went back home and was elected governor of Maine before settling in as Bowdoin's president.

From personal experience, he knew that almost anyone can rise to be a hero, and such people often can't even explain why. "Heroism is latent in every human soul . . . however humble and unknown," he said in a moving Memorial Day address in 1897, speaking of his fellow war veterans living and dead.

These are words to live by. Just open your eyes. You will find your own heroes—around the corner and around the world. Follow the examples they set. Make them your own. Before you know it, people will be looking to you as a hero.

TRIDENT TAKEAWAYS

➤ Heroes turn up in unexpected places.

➤ Heroes are never perfect—allow for that.

➤ Choose your own heroes by the qualities you admire.

CHAPTER 2

LESSONS FROM THE BROTHERHOOD

What makes the SEAL teams unique? A lot of things. Recruiting the right people. Training them, training them, and training them. Limiting the mission to things the teams are good at. Creating an unbreakable sense of brotherhood. It's all of that and this: our do-or-die refusal to fail. That's the ethic, so embedded in the Navy SEAL culture, that gathers mere mortals and sends them out as lethal killing machines. This refusal to fail applies far beyond the battlefield. This culture can be duplicated to a great extent in business, home, and political life.

SEAL POWER FLOWS FROM OUR UNIQUE HISTORY

Navy SEALs have a unique way of looking at warfare and at ourselves, derived from decades of constant training and grueling battle. But the lessons we've learned have applications far beyond the battlefield.

It all goes back to our earliest days. The year was 1962. The conflict in Vietnam was just getting serious. The war hadn't become a major national obsession, as it would in the later years of the decade. But the Viet Cong guerrillas were already causing headaches with their unconventional fighting techniques. They didn't wear traditional uniforms, sleep in large barracks, or launch their operations from fortified compounds. Sometimes, they coordinated with the regular North Vietnamese army, sometimes not. They faded in and out of the civilian population almost imperceptibly, then pounced with extraordinary violence against our South Vietnamese allies and their U.S. advisers before quickly slipping away again. There were some unavoidable parallels with America's experience in our own Revolutionary War against the British, but we weren't on the fun side this time.

America's armed forces hadn't had much recent experience with guerrilla-style warfare, and it showed. But some forward-thinking war planners around Washington, in contact with CIA and Army advisers on the ground, urged President John Kennedy to consider establishing an unconventional fighting force of our own.

He agreed.

The same day he vowed to send a spacecraft to the moon,

President Kennedy also directed the U.S. military to create small, elite units that were adept at unconventional warfare, though no one at the beginning was precisely certain what that might mean. Representing the Navy in this initiative were the Sea, Air and Land teams, or SEALs as they became known. Yes, the military does love its acronyms. For a brief while, these special warriors were called the Navy Black Berets, a reference to the legendary Army special-operations unit known as the Green Berets. Thankfully, that didn't stick. The SEALs' specialty: high-impact clandestine missions that the larger forces with their ships, tanks, jets, and submarines were not remotely built to handle. The SEALs were expected to work with Big Navy, the Marines, and the Army, conducting reconnaissance of critical targets, for example, and making underwater harbor maps in advance of amphibious landings. But mostly, they were encouraged to operate on their own. That meant all kinds of things: patrolling hostile territory, conducting lightning raids, taking on various missions that required unique flexibility and a more nimble approach. And while the SEALs were part of the Navy and much of their training was in or near the sea, from the very beginning they embraced the air and land as well, pointing out that *A* and *L* made up half of the acronym that formed their nickname.

None of these differences made the SEALs especially popular with America's conventional military leadership.

There was more than a little grumbling from hidebound generals and admirals inside the Pentagon. This flexibility, independence, and self-direction sounded mostly like trouble to them. Weren't strict discipline and order cornerstones of the military? Was it really wise to have a bunch of headstrong warriors, as the old guard put it, "running around on their own"? Those were the kinds of skeptical questions being asked. President Kennedy thought that was exactly what America needed, and he was commander in chief.

Indeed, the whole idea of the SEAL teams was that the old assumptions and rules should not necessarily apply to these elite units, and the SEALs took their independence to heart. They didn't need a road map to the war zone or the big military's approach to combat. They had the training. They had the confidence. SEALs knew they would figure it out as they went along.

The SEALs weren't entirely alone in this. The Green Berets, Marine Recon, Army Rangers, and special-operations units in other branches shared some of the SEALs' attributes and attitudes. Like us, they appreciated the powerful weaponry and massive troop strength that America's conventional forces brought to the war zone. Also like us, they recognized that all that force, which had been so effective during World War I and World War II, didn't apply as aptly to a guerrilla struggle in the rice paddies of Southeast Asia. An enemy you can't locate cannot be pounded with artillery, and the Viet Cong were simultaneously nowhere and everywhere. Fresh conditions require fresh responses. The age of overwhelming troop strength was giving way to the age of small, nimble, and quick.

Most of the skeptical admirals and generals eventually came around. They reluctantly accepted the proposition that the war zone was changing, perhaps forever, even if they didn't like or entirely understand the job we were trying to do. That shift didn't happen right away, but ultimately they decided they needed what it was we were promising to accomplish. Captain Phil Bucklew, commander of the Navy's special-operations mission at the time, put it in terms the top leadership could understand: "We are using the Viet Cong's hit-and-run tactics to harass them as much as they harass us." Bucklew was a warrior of unquestioned credibility who had twice earned the Navy Cross in World War II.

When SEAL Team One and SEAL Team Two hit the ground in Vietnam, they made their presence felt immediately. They were quick and crafty. Some people thought they were a little crazy. The SEALs seemed to know their way around. They were every bit as violent and relentless as the Viet Cong rebels. They launched hit-and-run air assaults using Army and Navy helicopters. They carried out day and night ambushes, though they much preferred the night. They found the names of guerrilla leaders and went looking for them.

The SEALs' reputation spread quickly. Some people said they had superhuman powers. That wasn't true, of course. They just had better training, more drive, and fewer rules. The Viet Cong were clearly frightened of them, offering bounties for the kill or capture of U.S. Navy SEALs, calling them "the men with green faces," a nod to the facial camouflage that they wore.

I hate the term *thinking outside the box*. It is overused and often applied to thinking that isn't remotely creative or unconventional. Though we never used that expression, the same basic idea was baked deeply into the culture of the SEAL teams. We were expected to do whatever it took—let me repeat that, *whatever* it took—to achieve victory in our missions. Any strategy. Any alliance. Any legal technique. And failure was not an option, period.

That attitude—and the training and culture that supported it—played a significant role in changing the modern battlefield and making America dominant against enemies large and small. It is almost unthinkable that the United States would go to war now without its esteemed special operators. And standing at the fore of the heroic line are today's 2,500 freewheeling, hard-driving, creative-thinking, failure-refusing U.S. Navy SEALs. Today, you don't hear too much grumbling about the SEALs from the brass at the Pentagon. You hear only pleas: How can we make more of you guys?

But what if we could take some of the lessons we have learned as special operators and apply them universally? What have we learned at war that civilian leaders might benefit from? What is important and what is not? Put it this way: Is there a special sauce in what SEALs do that could be spread around more broadly?

IT ALL STARTS WITH RECRUITING THE RIGHT PEOPLE

There is no one prototype SEAL, but there are certain kinds of people we always seek. People who are strong mentally and physically, able to withstand the toughest rigors of the battlefield and not collapse under pressure. People who are resilient. People who have the natural talent and open-mindedness to learn new skills. People who are different from one another—physically, temperamentally, intellectually. We also need people with their egos under control. We are SEAL *teams* for a reason. We are not solo cowboys, doing whatever we feel like. Teamwork is what makes us so effective. The team always comes first.

This high-demand approach to recruiting isn't relevant only to elite military units. It's just as appropriate in civilian life. Dedication, talent, diversity, teamwork: these are vital concepts in any organization with difficult, important work to do, whether a large corporation, a small business, or a non-profit group. No team will ever thrive if it's made up of the wrong people. That's a lesson we have learned very well in the SEAL teams.

Once assembled, our young SEAL pups need to be trained. And trained and trained and trained some more. Trained to the point of exhaustion, sometimes trained within an inch of their lives. From the first day of basic training until a grizzly veteran puts his retirement papers in, the training does not end. We know from experience we will send these warriors into high-stress, high-danger situations, where their lives and the lives of their teammates will depend on how well they perform. Nothing replaces constant, repetitive training. You can take the most macho, self-confident warrior who has ever stepped out on a battlefield, and he will perform unreliably if he isn't trained thoroughly and correctly. When the bullets start flying, a trained warrior doesn't hesitate. He just reacts. There is no amount of natural talent that isn't improved by performing each critical act thousands of times in preparation. That's what we do in SEAL training, then we do it another few thousand times.

Again, this commitment to hypertraining echoes its way clearly into civilian life, though the specific regimen would have to be different for different careers. Outside of the military, no one could get away with some of the harsher training techniques we use. Imagine the reaction if Goldman Sachs told its next class of recruits that they should paddle inflatable boats through gut-wrenching surf, stand for an hour in fifty-five-degree seawater, haul logs the size of telephone poles across a broad expanse of beach front, then take a quick chow break cross-legged in the prickly sand. Morgan Stanley could expect a sudden rush of lateral-transfer applications! The *New York Times* would immediately investigate, and the Securities and Exchange Commission wouldn't be far behind. But training is just as crucial on Wall Street as it is in Iraq's Anbar Province.

BUILD THE RIGHT STRUCTURE FOR YOUR TEAM

Structure matters too. Finding the right people and training them intensely will be a waste if you don't have the right command structure in place. Our SEAL team spirit is legendary. But we are still a military organization with a rank structure, officers, and enlisted personnel. Everyone reports to someone, straight up to the commander in chief. But we interact differently than most military organizations do.

Early on, our SEAL forefathers realized that if our guys were required to sport the usual high-and-tight military haircuts and spit-polished boots, they'd be prone to rank-and-file attitudes—not at all conducive to creative thinking. I know people have job titles in corporate America, but that isn't quite the same. If a senior executive steps into the mailroom, the mailroom staff will certainly take notice. But it doesn't have the impact of a four-star admiral walking into a Navy-base chow hall filled with enlisted personnel. That's a very big thing. People come to attention. You can feel the excitement or apprehension in the air. People may wonder, "What's he doing here?" But in deference to the superior rank he carries, almost certainly no one will ask him.

This tradition of the officer as an unquestioned god wasn't going to work in this new type of fighting force. Yes to respect. Yes to a clear chain of command. But no to the usual military culture, where the guy actually doing the fighting is treated as a grunt no one wants to hear from. This could not be the SEAL way or bring us the flexible, creative, lethal thinking we knew we needed to succeed. So we devised a different way.

The SEAL community has the rank structure of any other military organization—we just live those relationships differently. We have enlisted men from seaman recruit to master chief, and officers from ensign to admiral. The orders go down, not up. That said, the relationship between officers and those enlisted in the SEAL teams accommodates far more give-and-take than any other military unit. A captain and his master chief, or a platoon commander and his platoon chief, are on a much more even plane than comparable ranks anywhere else. Our guys question authority far more than would ever be acceptable in other traditional military organizations. SEALs are far quicker to challenge a leader directly.

Undisciplined isn't the right way to describe this. It's just that our culture is less rigid. We are more familiar with one another and talk in a much more candid manner than you would hear between officers and enlisted personnel in the 4th Infantry Division. The buck private in the 4th Infantry Division is most likely not going to give his frank opinion to a major, especially about an operational decision the major has made. There would be so much deference and so many "sirs," the major might never discover what the private really thought. A lieutenant commander and an enlisted SEAL—the parallel ranks on a SEAL team—would relate far more openly. On SEAL teams, everyone is heard. For us, open communication is the watchword, shamelessly thumbing our noses at Frederick the Great's famous comment about his troops: "If my soldiers were to begin to think, not one would remain in the ranks."

Sorry, Fred. We're not in Prussia, and it's not the eighteenth century anymore.

If an enlisted SEAL thinks his lieutenant commander is screwing up, believe me, he'll let the officer know. He will do it with respect. He won't just say, "You idiot." But he will say, "No, no, no, that's not a good idea. Here's why." The comment may not alter the decision or change the lieutenant commander's mind. But the junior man can expect that his input will at least be considered and he won't face retaliation for speaking up.

I don't want to overstate this. The decision is still the officer's in the end. And the enlisted SEAL is expected to follow orders, even if he personally disagrees. But this back-and-forth is very valuable to us. It brings in new data and encourages independent thinking—up and down the ranks. It goes a long way toward making the SEALs the creative fighting force we are. Our very purpose for being, after all, was to look at war through fresh and open eyes.

SOMEONE HAS TO BE IN CHARGE

Our unique SEAL openness also causes some problems. There's no denying that. Simple rules are easier to follow, but our relationships are a bit more nuanced. Sometimes, the easy rapport can erode command authority, especially when a leader isn't as clearheaded or self-confident as he should be. As a group, SEAL commanders are extraordinary individuals. But they are human beings too. Misunderstandings do pop up.

As my last platoon was preparing to leave for Iraq, a group of us started a small fight club. We'd get up at 4 a.m. Before we went off to our daily combat exercises, we'd train in Brazilian jujitsu. A couple of guys were exceptional at it, so they took on the role of instructors. There were officers and enlisted guys all thrown in together. This was hand-to-hand combat and had nothing to do with rank. Rank just disappeared once we were fighting. There was no other way to do it, truthfully. Can you imagine an officer telling an enlisted SEAL, "Oh, you can't hit me that hard—I outrank you"? That's not the way we do it. We train hard with everybody. SEALs all being naturally competitive, everyone tried to win every match.

All things considered, I would say our fight club was mostly problem free. But we're still human. Every once in a while, our easy camaraderie became an issue. If you had a bone to pick with someone, regardless of rank, it would sometimes play out in our fights. There came a flashpoint for me. It was something significant, trivial though it seemed, and I felt I needed to react. Early one morning, a couple of months in, one of my junior enlisted men came up to me in our locker room and said: "Hey, Rorke. Let me ask you something."

He had never called me "Rorke" before.

I didn't insist I always be addressed as "lieutenant." Most of the guys called me "LT" or sometimes "Mr. D"—but never just my first name. And I have to say, I was slightly taken aback.

"What did you say?" I asked him.

He must have noticed something in my tone, and caught himself, looking slightly surprised by my reaction. I guess I'd made clear I wasn't pleased. We were getting up early and using our personal time to do this extra training, which was fine, I thought. But I sensed it might have taken us a little too far outside the disciplined team environment.

"I want to make sure I'm clear about this," I went on, "so you understand where I'm coming from. You calling me 'sir' or 'lieutenant' does nothing for my ego. I don't need to hear it or be saluted to feel good about myself. But when you call me by my first name, I think it's actually a representation of you, not me. It conflicts with our discipline structure and relationship in this professional environment. Now I'm not saying I think you're less than what I thought of you yesterday. But I can tell you assuredly that the enlisted guys on the team who understand these lines are the ones everyone else will consider the most squared away. As an officer, I can tell you that when you have a guy that always maintains military bearing and discipline, you can't help but think, 'That guy has it together.'"

The junior man just looked at me. He didn't say anything. I was hoping he was absorbing this, not just feeling lectured. I looked him square in the face and went on.

"So when you call me 'Rorke,' it makes me think you don't have it together. It makes me think you don't care about my position and you don't care about your position and the discipline that goes along with that."

I wasn't done yet.

"Bigger than that," I said, "when we go over to Iraq, if you call me that in front of a Marine or a Marine unit, they're going to think we're absolute clowns. That is a bridge too far. It's one thing for you to call me a nickname here, but when we're around the joint ranges, you should just call me 'LT' because our sister units need to hear that."

Despite all the advantages of looseness and flexibility on a well-functioning team, rank and authority do still have their place in the world, on and off the battlefield. This should be understood by civilian CEOs, moms, and community leaders, as it is by military commanders.

"In the lunchroom or brainstorming sessions, we welcome a freewheeling back-and-forth," a corporate leader may tell her team. "But when we go into the meeting with the client, we speak with one voice, and it's mine."

NEVER QUIT, NO MATTER WHAT

This matters more than anything. Of all the things worth exporting from SEAL culture, nothing is more valuable than our adamant refusal to quit. It's top, hands down. It's what separates our boys from everyone else on the battlefield and in most of society. The people who make it through SEAL training never had any quit in them and never will.

It's the main reason our on-ramp is so steep. It is designed to make people quit, and it is highly effective at doing so. Seventy-five to 80 percent of the young men who show up for BUD/S (Basic Underwater Demolition/SEAL)—our initial six-month training program—do not make it through. At some point between the grueling beach runs, wild boat races, frigid water, sleeplessness, and aptly named Hell Week, most SEAL recruits come to a personal realization. "You know," they say to themselves, "this really isn't for me." The vast majority aren't kicked out or asked to leave. They weigh the dire circumstances they find themselves in and decide on their own they are done. They DOR, drop on request. The young man walks into an open courtyard at our training compound on Coronado Island off San Diego. There, he rings the bell three times, signaling to everyone within earshot that someone else has called it quits. He then places his helmet at the end of a row of helmets left by other young men who made the same decision, and he is gone.

There is no shame in any of this. We don't have the young lions ring the bell to embarrass them. That is not what it's about. It's an acknowledgment of how hard this training is and how hard they have found it to be. The SEAL teams aren't for everyone. Most of these young men will go on to serve in other ways and lead highly productive lives. We wish them well. They just won't be SEALs.

If this sounds like a high barrier to entry, it is. It is designed—unapologetically—to ensure that many people leave and, more to the point, that the right people stay.

But the guys who stick it out despite all we put them through, I swear they have a near-irrational belief in their own abilities and a total refusal to fold. They are truly convinced nothing can stop them. And believe in their hearts that, whatever mission they are asked to accomplish, they, and their teammates, will be up to the task. Failure is not an option. It's not even an imaginable possibility.

Franklin Delano Roosevelt had a great way of describing this attitude. "When you come to the end of your rope," the four-term American president said, "tie a knot and hang on." No one ever accused FDR of giving up too soon.

Do you have any idea how powerful a spirit like that can be? These special men aren't just giving lip service. We aren't just *playing* SEAL. We live and breathe that stubborn commitment to our core. It is real because we believe it is real. If you doubt me, just try telling us we are wrong.

That refusal to quit is the single most important quality that our training and culture instill. More important than the ability to plant explosives, plan a dangerous mission, or shoot with extreme precision. With sufficient practice, most people can develop those skills. The lack of quit has to rise from within.

I have noticed over the years that there are a few recruits who arrive at BUD/S and surprise themselves by surviving. They are not sure if they can handle it, but they do. That is inspiring to witness. Far more recruits arrive thinking they can, and don't. But most of the guys I was closest to in BUD/S didn't, for even a moment, have a shred of doubt that they would make it through, and most did. That's how I felt too. There was nothing the instructors were going to throw at us that would convince us otherwise. There was no exhaustion or discomfort that was going to break us. They could turn Hell Week into Hell Month. Unless it killed us, we weren't going anywhere. It was almost like we were daring the instructors: "Give it your best shot." They did, and we prevailed. We were the guys they were looking for.

Being that close to making it, pushed like never before, I was being accepted in the place I wanted to be the most—a place that could offer me adventure, excitement, and the ability to test everything I wanted to test about myself. And I was surrounded by a bunch of other guys who felt exactly the same way. They couldn't have pulled me out of there with a crowbar and a pack of mules. All I needed to do was refuse to quit.

I know that might sound trite. It could be the slogan on a poster hung on some teenager's bedroom wall. But it's one of the most compelling forces that drives the SEAL community—and it could be just as potent in almost any competitive environment.

I catch glimpses of this winning attitude in civilian life every now and then, and not always in the places you'd expect. I feel it when I phone USAA, a private insurance company that caters to the military. I dare you to call these people and not have them impress you with their unparalleled customer service. They don't even seem to mind if I call with a claim on my policy. Truly, they seem to do whatever it takes to make the policy owner happy, and will not stop until they do.

You never know where this stubborn winning attitude will shine through. Chick-fil-A isn't the only fast-food chain with tasty food, but it's unbeatable when it comes to having a predictably winning attitude. Its employees refuse to let you leave unhappy. In my experience, other chains accomplish that at some locations on some days, but I have never known Chick-fil-A to fail.

As with the SEALs, recruiting is undoubtedly part of the success of these two businesses. But at its base, it's a cultural thing—instilled in the DNA of the organization. The message goes out in both companies from leadership to the employees on the front lines. It's a strong and pervasive ethic that says: we do whatever it takes to get the job done right.

I don't know all the details, but I know this much: The make-it-work attitude has developed inside those organizations through a process not so different from what we do as SEALs.

That kind of culture and attitude can beat integrity, decency, vision, humility, and all manner of other powerful attributes. Do the right thing. Just keep going and do not stop—no matter what. The no-matter-what part is crucial. If others think they can wear you down, they will make every effort to do just that. If you believe and let them know it is not a possibility, they too will eventually accept that as fact.

There were times in Anbar Province when we certainly had every reason to give up. Everyone seemed to be against us. Criticism of the war was rising at home. Our allied Iraqi troops weren't remotely ready to fight. We were the "occupiers from America." As deeply divided as Iraq was, there was one thing its many factions, including our supposed friends, seemed to agree on: we had little business being there and no business staying for any length of time. But we came with a job to do, and we were determined to do it.

When we first got there, small teams of Sunni fighters were driving around with three-pronged mortar tubes on the beds of small Toyota trucks, blasting away at American targets with near impunity. We knew immediately that could not stand.

We SEALs got busy as soon as we settled into our compound. We studied the situation and tried to figure out what our predecessors might have been missing. We hatched a plan we knew would be risky—nighttime patrol in the worst of what we called "Indian country"—and we went looking for the bad guys on their own turf. I think Sunni fighters were shocked the first few times we turned up. We were armed—and ready. We were where we weren't supposed to be. We hit with overwhelming force. And it worked. The bad guys didn't throw up their hands and surrender, but the SEALs made it known we were there to win. This changed the dynamic on the ground.

It wasn't just us. There were other special operators who approached the challenges on the ground from a similar mind-set, refusing to quit. Together, our aggressive missions helped to spark what became known as the Sunni Awakening in western Iraq. It marked a real turning point in that difficult struggle and helped policy makers in Washington, including President George W. Bush, justify a large troop surge. Our refusal to quit helped turn a losing operation around.

What was accomplished in Iraq went back to something instilled in us during Hell Week. BUD/S is tough from day one, but it truthfully is about Hell Week in the end. If you can make it through that, chances are you are going to become a Navy SEAL. After that brutal week, there is almost nothing you and your teammates can't achieve. You believe it, and it is effective.

MY PERSONAL NO-QUIT MANIFESTO

I had a speech I liked to give when I was running basic training. I gave it right before Hell Week to every single class. "If nothing else," I would say, "don't throw in the towel. Just keep sweating. Just keep slugging. If you just do that, you're going to get way further than you imagined and way further than you would have had you given up. As soon as you give up on yourself, it's over. You're done. I'm not saying you have to be a SEAL. Whatever it is in life, this applies. Whether you wake up one morning and say, 'I want to write a novel,' or 'I've always wanted to be a painter,' or 'I want to walk across the country,' or 'I want to build my own house'—whatever it is, if you don't give up, you are likely to achieve it. It is almost never just about your ability or your contacts or the family you were born into. It's about how much quit lies inside of you."

And then the kicker:

"If you quit this, if you quit anything that is important to you, you are one hundred percent certain not to realize that dream."

It's a stark realization and an undeniable fact, enforced for all of us by the unique SEAL brotherhood.

One of the reasons I know the guy on my right and the guy on my left are the guys I want next to me is I know they are not going to quit. Period. The alternative is just unacceptable. How would it be, when the shooting starts in a gunfight, to look to your left—he's still shooting—then look to your right and he's fled the scene? When you are out there fighting with SEALs, that's not a concern. Maybe it's what has been drilled into us, or maybe it's the way we were born.

By the time a young SEAL experiences his first firefight, we know everything there is to know about that guy. We know he's looking out for his brothers first and foremost, and we know with certainty that he isn't going to quit.

Isn't that the kind of person anyone would want to take into a gunfight?

I am often asked by young men who dream of joining the SEAL teams: What can I do to get in? Is there some course of study or some exercise program or some diet or some something that will improve the odds? It would be easy for me to tell them to set up some logs on the beach or start spending time in frigidly cold water, but I'm not sure any of that would help. I know the real gauntlet our recruits must get through is mental. It isn't physical at all.

"It's the spirit," I tell them. "You've got to find the spirit. That's what will get you through." Without that spirit, an understandable desire to quit can creep up. We set up opportunities—mental and physical challenges—to figure out if the candidates are ready or not.

And if the new recruits never give in to the temptation to DOR, if they find that grit inside themselves and grind through to the end, we know they have something special. We know they're the kind of guys you want with you in a battle with an enemy intent on killing you. We know one thing for certain. We know they will find a way to prevail.

One of the great joys of SEAL training is that you know what happens if you don't quit. You get to be a SEAL.

Later on, the demands will get more technical. SEALs train like crazy in various specialties. You'll become a breacher, sniper, radio operator, or an explosives expert. If you took the officer track, you'll grow into a succession of leadership posts. Based on individual talents, temperament, and the needs of the teams, this will be sorted out as time goes on.

At their core, SEALs are problem solvers, modern warriors who will be expected to perform in some of the most challenging environments on earth. Technical skill, creative thinking, clear vision, selflessness, team spirit, and strong leadership can all be honed with training and experience. The part we can't manufacture, the part you have to bring from home, is the character that keeps you going and the refusal to ever stop short of success.

None of this is meant as a prescription for martyrdom. Winning is a big part of the SEAL equation, and sometimes winning takes time and thought. So we don't preach, "Never retreat under any circumstances." Sometimes, retreating momentarily is the better part of valor. There are times when a SEAL officer has to direct his men: "Let's get the hell out of here—and fast!" When that order comes, you want teammates who are going to pull out and then regroup to fight another day.

Through it all, there's a voice inside that keeps saying, "I will find a way to meet this challenge . . . I am here for my teammates . . . I will not fail no matter what." That voice is never silent. You are a SEAL.

Let everyone know: "What we do matters . . . We perform superbly . . . We don't quit . . . If you aren't good enough, you don't get to stay . . . You are here, so you must be great."

We have learned a lot from our wild SEAL history and our many adventures over the years. Along with our God-given talents and our powerful brotherhood, those are the source of all we are today. Duplicate that confident belief inside any organization, and it will become unstoppable.

TRIDENT TAKEAWAYS

➤ Embrace the culture that works for you.

➤ Success has many pathways.

➤ Just don't quit.

CHAPTER 3

HOW TO BE BRAVE

I always knew I wanted to be a father, and I was certain I'd have no trouble handling boys. I grew up with a younger brother. I had lots of male cousins and friends. I was a competitive athlete in high school and college on the water polo and lacrosse teams. I loved to surf, hunt, fish, and engage in other traditionally male activities. When it came time to pick a career, I joined the Navy SEALs, which I like to describe as "the greatest man club on earth."

But God threw me a curve ball, and I knew I had to hit it out of the park.

In the course of two years, my superstar bride, Tracy, and I were blessed with two beautiful little girls. And I take my role seriously in raising them.

Now, *that* requires bravery. To be perfectly frank about it, I never felt more frightened of anything in my life.

I had free-fallen from airplanes. I had survived dozens of gunfights. I had led small teams of warriors down some of the scariest roads on earth. None of it prepared me for this, being personally responsible for the lives of these two precious little girls.

Girls are different. They have emotions I can't possibly fathom. They are vulnerable in all kinds of mysterious ways. And these two seem to notice everything I do. Girls are far harder on one another than boys ever will be. Two boys can get in a fistfight, and five minutes later, they are joking together in the school yard. It's all so much more complicated with girls. I was hugely grateful I married such a savvy partner in crime, who I knew would be an over-the-moon great mom. None of this seemed to stress Tracy.

When my friends who have sons give me encouragement or advice, I just look at them and shake my head: "Brother, you have boys. You have no idea."

When some clueless idiot asks, "So, you gonna keep trying until you get a boy," my answer turns three shades darker: "God only sends girls to the real men. I'm blessed to have them."

Around the girls, I know, I have to be the best possible embodiment of manhood. I don't want them getting the wrong ideas about what men are. God knows who they might decide to bring home fifteen years from now. I want to instill in my daughters virtues and behaviors that will serve them well as they get older. I want to expose them to all the wonders of the world, and not just the traditional girlie ones. They might grow up loving to fish, hunt, or repair diesel engines. Either way, I have to remember to let them decide.

I knew from the start this mission was going to require some serious guts. It has.

Not long ago, the younger one had a challenge at school with a bully in kindergarten. I remember being bullied as a kid and how tough it was for me. I remember how my family encouraged me to handle situations like that one. But at five years old, she seemed a little young for me to be teaching her jujitsu. I could have. I'm experienced, and she's capable. But I haven't. I don't think she's quite ready to put anyone's lights out in the school yard. I'm not sure her teacher is ready for that either. There's also the question of escalating a classroom dynamic into something larger, which I could do by orchestrating a way to run into the dad somewhere and having a conversation with him. I haven't done that either. In my heart, I know it's better for my daughter to learn to stand up for herself—and to learn it on her own, gradual timetable. This is a strange, new outlook for a SEAL officer who is trained to be there always in any way necessary for everyone on my team.

What can I tell you? Having daughters is a master class in emotional intensity that I frequently think I might fail.

Fortunately, I had learned a thing or two about facing my fears. From the many other dicey situations I'd found myself in, I had built my bravery muscles. I knew expertise would come with practice. I knew confidence was something I could stoke. I knew, ready or not, I would have to dive in.

This whole father-of-girls thing is still a work in progress. But I might be okay at it in the end. Ask my daughters twenty years from now.

PRACTICE MAKES BRAVERY

Almost nobody is born brave. At war or at home, bravery has to be learned.

Some people have natural inclinations in that direction. They have strong impulse control and clear field vision, and their hearts don't race at the first hint of danger. Those characteristics provide fertile ground for bravery to grow. But real bravery is something that can be—that must be—coaxed out of all of us.

I've heard heart-pumping stories that would make you believe otherwise. They pop up every now and then, coming out of nowhere and ending up on the evening news. The local minister who stands between armed police and armed rioters. The quiet neighbor who rushes into a burning house and pulls a sleeping family out of bed. Desperation and drive can be powerful motivators. Panic can too.

But those cases are lightning strikes, rare and unpredictable, even as they light up the sky with brilliant colors. Bravery is far more often something that builds up gradually. Practice comes in handy no matter what. It improves the success rate and ups the odds. Wouldn't you rather have a trained first responder running into your burning bedroom instead of a caring neighbor, no matter how well intentioned he or she might be? Bravery isn't a muscle, but it might as well be. The more it's used, the stronger it will be.

The SEALs are living proof of that.

When we were young most of us were no braver than the other kids. Okay, maybe a little—but that's not what sets us apart. It's that all of us have trained for years in activities that required copious amounts of bravery. We got braver slowly before we ever stepped into a genuine combat zone, where bullets fly and bombs go off. Before we were deployed anywhere, we practiced in situations in which the demands and then the danger were real. Hard-fought war games in dense jungles and mountainous terrain. High-risk, free-fall parachute jumps. Complex assaults on compounds defended by other SEALs. Underwater challenges like having your scuba lines tied into knots while a sinister chief wrestles you in the deep end of the pool. It takes quite a few rounds of those all-too-real simulations to start building your confidence and technique. Believe me, I was a whole lot calmer the hundredth time I jumped out of a plane than I was the first time.

Then we put all that training into practice in real war zones. And we do that over and over again. Raiding a house where we know the inhabitants are armed and waiting. Exercising good judgment is part of what's necessary. In a situation like that, there are things you do and don't do. You pick a time when you think the people might be sleeping or distracted. You approach quietly. Without warning, you kick in the door or blow it off the hinges with a well-placed explosive charge. You rush inside with a sudden roar of aggression, betting you can subdue the people before they have an instant to react. Even with the best planning and execution, there is danger. You have to stay calm. You have to think strategically. You have to be aware of your teammates at all times. You have to strike without reluctance and not hold back. And even so, the mission requires bravery because you are risking your life and those of your teammates by just being there.

But the best way to increase the odds is practice—two kinds of practice, actually. Practicing the immediate techniques for better mastery and practicing the psychology of being brave. Together, they are the best a warrior can do.

Because we practice so often, literally every man in every SEAL class will become brave. There isn't a mathematical scale like on a blood-pressure gauge or a thermometer to measure this process. But if there were, all these guys would be in the hundredth percentile for bravery.

Hollywood keeps arguing against that, constantly trying to convince us that bravery springs up almost miraculously on its own. Today's action-adventure movies are more like comic books. In fact, more and more box office hits are actually made *from* comic books. Superheroes keep swooping down at the very last minute and performing death-defying rescues—because, you know, that's just who they are. In Hollywood, bravery is portrayed as an innate human characteristic, a trait you're either born with or you're not, and some people are blessed with heaping helpings of it. Well, real life isn't Mark Wahlberg, Chris Hemsworth, Vin Diesel, or Superman. Real heroes aren't born heroic. Most get there gradually, by practicing little acts of bravery. They are regular human beings who have made the commitment over time to be brave.

If you want to learn to be brave, you need to put yourself in scenarios that require boldness. Whatever your field of endeavor, whether you're a solider, a homemaker, or a business executive—you have chances to exercise your bravery muscles every day. You have to start seizing those opportunities, no matter how small they are at first. Speak up in a meeting where other people disagree with you. Lift more than you thought you were able to at the gym. Eat a dish you were certain you'd hate the taste of. You might even surprise yourself.

On the long road to world-changing bravery, these are certainly baby steps. But they will get you moving and put you into the mind-set of doing things you are scared of. And that's a pretty good rough definition of what it means to be brave.

Omar Bradley served as a five-star general during World War II and had the longest military service in U.S. history, performing and witnessing many acts of courage. He famously said, "Bravery is the capacity to perform properly even when scared half to death." From fatherhood to knife fights, that's as good a description as any I've heard.

It's been proven over and over: before we get good at anything, we have do it a few times—or even a few thousand. If you want to be brave, you must practice. Practice manages fear, practice sharpens performance, practice builds self-confidence. Any one of those three can be lifesaving in a gunfight, but they will also make you braver in everyday life at the office or walking down the street.

Danger creates fear in any rational human being, including a trained warrior. That kind of fear can chisel you down to the bone. It strips people raw. But if you can properly channel it, fear can also help you find your true self.

HOW TO BEAT BACK THE FEAR

Managing fear, sharpening performance, building confidence: the SEALs know this process well. Our training is based directly on these concepts. In the military, we create scenarios and training programs that attempt to replicate the most intense moments of the battlefield. What we are doing as SEALs or in other branches of the military requires us to go against a lot of basic human instincts. When natural caution says, "Get out of there," we go in. We run *to* the sound of the guns. SEALs don't run away.

Fear never entirely leaves. That wouldn't be desirable even if you could make it happen. The fear helps you focus and keeps you alert. Fear offers enlightenment to those who are willing to face and deal with it.

There's no better way to be prepared for a situation that makes you afraid than to face your fears repeatedly. Think of the constant repetition like a powerful inoculation against some dreaded disease. Take a little now. You'll be ready the next time it comes around.

The first time I was in a gunfight wasn't the first time I was in a gunfight. I had run the scenario hundreds of times in practice. Physically, yes. But emotionally and mentally too. I'd learned that managing my fear was just as important a part of a gunfight as knowing how to pick the right ammunition. Through constant repetition, I learned that in a gunfight, the heart races, the adrenaline pumps hard, the mind bounces like a pinball. I learned that in fear-packed circumstances, instinct could lead me to stand up, step out from behind cover, and do something stupid that would give the enemy a clear shot—and I didn't want to do any of that. With all that practice, I learned that it's often the panic that gets you killed. Practice taught me that the way to survive and win a gunfight was to stay as calm, focused, and strategic as possible. And the way I learned that—truly learned it— wasn't from a book or an instruction manual or even one of the godlike instructors who supervised our SEAL training. It was from practicing gunfights a couple of thousand times. I remained highly respectful of the risks involved—I just wasn't rattled by them anymore.

I got a lot of fear-management training when I was growing up. Sports, we called it. Junior high football, high school water polo, Division I lacrosse in college—these are all combative team sports. The pressure level might have been a notch or two below what the pros face, or what I confronted in battle, though I have to say, those youthful contests seemed mighty important at the time.

In every one of those arenas, there were high-pressure moments. Essentially, you have an hour to prove yourself. You are competing against another team that has that same hour to beat you. Inevitably, in a good game, there are a few special moments of elevated stress—if you haven't experienced this as an athlete, then you've certainly felt it as a fan watching a close game on TV. The clock is ticking down. The buzzer is about to sound. Did he get the shot off in time? He did! It went in! Or did it? It won the game! Or did it miss and we lose? Sports provide frequent opportunities for that high-pressure experience.

Because of sports, the highs and lows and the adrenaline rush were not unfamiliar to me when I started training for war, training for much-higher-stakes live combat. The intense pressure felt familiar to me. It was something I was very much at ease with. I learned to perform inside those moments during my time as an athlete, knowing I could affect the outcome, leading my teammates and also depending on them—all of us together tasting glorious victory and heartbreaking defeat.

There's a lot going on in these games that athletes play. Physical skill is only a part of it. Competition is just as much a mental exercise. Learning to manage stress, staying focused, and remaining sharp instead of shutting down. Sports that children and students participate in have become the focus of much criticism in our culture today. Some of it is even justified. But competitive team sports are also a wonderful teacher. Frankly, I don't know where I'd be without them.

When I faced genuine danger on the battlefield, the feelings were already familiar. I'd had the practice necessary to conquer them, and I had a lot of athletic inoculation already running through my veins. The two worlds are very similar, as things turned out.

When you put yourself through tough times, you are preparing yourself for the tough times to come, whether you realize it or not. You become ready in every way possible. But being ready isn't enough for true bravery.

HOW TO GET GOOD AT BEING BRAVE

When I found myself in my first real gun battle with people who actually wanted to kill me, I had the ability to manage my fear because of all that practice. But beyond that, I also knew almost everything there was to know about gunfights. Through repetition, I had learned how to aim, how to reload a weapon in the dark, and how to be aware of my surroundings—the practical skills I needed to know.

You don't truly know how you'll perform in a dangerous situation until you're tested.

You can put yourself in scenarios where you actually get to experience those emotions and test them to see how you'd react. You can force yourself to do things that make you afraid or uncomfortable. If you have a major speech to give, try a short one in front of your friends first. If you dream of running a marathon, knock out a half-marathon as a practice run. If your friends have planned a big evening in a karaoke bar, work out the high notes in the shower to gain more confidence in your singing abilities.

Visualization also helps. Medical research has proven this. Scientists can check your brain waves and monitor your vital signs in controlled experiments. They gather data on your brain as it confronts an unfamiliar situation or one you've had a chance to go over repeatedly in your head. Familiarity breeds expertise. Practice and visualization, they are a potent combination. If you can combine the two, you've got a very powerful alchemy at your disposal.

There's a lot of science involved in why this works. There's also a tremendous amount of heart and mystery to it as well. High-stress environments shut some people down. For others, the stress turns them on, makes them sharper, and activates their receptors. It's usually one of those two things. The first reaction is far more common; stress, fear, and other life-and-death-type situations shut most people down. But some people—professional athletes, the best SEALs—thrive in high-stress, fear-filled moments.

CONFIDENCE SEALS THE BRAVERY

Performing acts of bravery also builds confidence. Far too much of our culture is focused on avoiding pain and living an easy life. There are people who glide through life, and as long as things are going well, everything is just wonderful. But once they hit a bump or things get really difficult, they're not prepared. They're not ready for that struggle. I had a SEAL teammate who was a real golden boy. He was a star in SEAL officer training. He was a top performer in his class based on run times, swim times, and the evaluations of the instructor cadre. He was a Ferrari. Fast, sleek—but a little temperamental. If he had good food and good sleep, he was unstoppable. But when he got to the real SEAL teams, they didn't always have good food. Sometimes, they went without proper sleep. Things got hard. Conditions got nasty. There were challenging people on the job. On the teams, the officers' job really is all about taking care of the boys under far-from-ideal circumstances.

The golden boy imploded. He was almost run out of the SEAL teams. He had natural talent and ability, but his life up to that point had just been too easy. He was smart, athletic, good-looking—one of those guys who looked like he just walked off an episode of *The Bachelor*. The SEALs could smell that, and they were instantly suspicious. The feeling was "No.

You're not our kind of guy." They made it harder on him, and he crumbled. He might have possessed all the right qualities for a SEAL, except the one that he'd never had to learn: staying strong under adverse conditions.

I saw this scenario occur quite a few times. It was always the guys who worked, struggled, and pushed through hardship who did really well. Struggle can be good. Failure can be good. It prepares you for when things get difficult. I learned far more as an athlete from the games I lost than from the games I won. It may be human nature for people to do everything in their power to avoid anything uncomfortable. But that's a mistake.

We live in plush houses. We spin around in high-performance luxury cars. We pass our days and nights, no matter what the climate or weather, in carefully controlled temperatures. We surround ourselves with laborsaving technologies and pleasant media distractions. Some people hardly walk to get anywhere. Almost everything can now be ordered online and delivered swiftly to our homes in less than twenty-four hours. The only sweating we experience, if any, happens on high-tech machines in sleek, well-lit gyms.

This is all perfectly understandable. It's not even inherently bad. Everyone wants to be comfortable. Luxury is pleasing. Pleasure is nicer than pain. But when we reach the point where we can no longer handle even the mildest of discomforts—when minor inconveniences start feeling like major catastrophes—something is out of whack, and we're much worse off for it. When this happens, we've gotten too soft. We haven't struggled enough in life, so we don't know how to struggle. People are losing the ability to do things that are hard. Eventually, we start to lose our belief in ourselves. We aren't prepared when difficulties arrive—and they inevitably do, no matter how swathed in comfort and protection we think we are.

Confidence comes with achieving things that challenge us. If we take all the difficulty away, how will we ever earn our self-confidence?

It sounds funny to say this, but I am hugely grateful that things didn't always come easily to me. I struggled academically from a very young age. Eventually, I was diagnosed with a learning disability. At the time, I definitely didn't enjoy having trouble in school, especially with math and science. It caused concern for my family and me. At times, it made me doubt myself. But that adversity turned out to be a giant gift to me, even though I didn't appreciate it until later in life. Because I worked hard and overcame some difficult challenges at a young age, I developed a muscle memory for hard work, and I had a real appreciation for the rewards of success. When things get tough now, I know how to push through. And I work my tail off, knowing how glad I'll be that I did.

If I didn't face what I did as a child, I'm not sure I would've developed this skill as effectively.

Practicing bravery is the world's greatest manager of fear, improver of performance, and builder of confidence. Don't go into any difficult situations without it. Take it from someone who's gone into more than a few.

TRIDENT TAKEAWAYS

➤ Do challenging things.

➤ Do them again.

➤ Practice plus confidence equals bravery.

CHAPTER 4

HOW TO KILL RIGHT

The Sixth Commandment certainly sounds unequivocal: "Thou shalt not kill." At first glance, these four words do not seem to contain much wiggle room. The New Testament doubles down on the idea that killing is a grave moral evil, as do the sacred texts of Islam, Hinduism, and virtually every other faith. Jesus was especially direct on this point. "You shall not murder," He says in Matthew 5:21. This is an imperative echoed in Matthew 19:19, Mark 10:19, Luke 18:20, and many other verses in the Gospels.

But I am in the killing business. All warriors are. Everything we do—every training exercise, strategic decision, and tactical move—serves the same eventual purpose, taking the lives of enemy combatants before they have an opportunity to take ours. Killing is what we are expected to do when the order is handed down to us, but there is nothing simple about it.

Even in the Bible, the prohibition against killing is nowhere near as airtight as it might at first sound. There are all kinds of exceptions to the no-killing rule, some of them wide enough to drive an armored personnel carrier through. While denouncing killing in general, almost every major religion recognizes the concept that killing can be justified in circumstances such as self-defense, capital punishment, and legitimate warfare. Warfare is the one I'm most interested in.

The Old Testament clearly sanctions killing in battle (Exodus 20:13, Exodus 34:10–14, Deuteronomy 7:7–26). One of David's men is celebrated for killing eight hundred men with his spear (2 Samuel 23:8). Abishai is credited with killing three hundred (2 Samuel 23:18). Young David is lauded as a hero for slaying the brutish Goliath in battle (1 Samuel 17). Along with many exhortations to the contrary ("Blessed are the meek" . . . "Turn the other cheek"), the New Testament is constantly referencing legitimate acts of war. Paul exhorts the Ephesians to "put on the full armor of God" (Ephesians 6). Cornelius, the Roman centurion, is portrayed as a righteous and God-fearing man (Acts 10). Jesus lavishly praises the faith of a Roman centurion while healing the centurion's servant (Luke 7:1–10).

So where does all this leave us, especially those who are sometimes called into battle and expected to perform? Killing, even for the noblest cause, raises many questions. Killing changes a man. It always does. Is it wrong to enjoy killing? Is it wrong to enjoy being in the theater of war? Can a killer enjoy his work and his home life? Can you be a professional killer and still be a loving husband, good father, and moral man? What does this all mean for the warrior's masculinity, mental health, and chances of returning as a healthy civilian?

Killing brings up many questions. We have to try to answer them.

Although we need to be effective warriors, we also need some principles for killing in a manner we can justify. Bible verses taken alone can be maddeningly opaque. That rough balance between the need to kill and the killer's humanity is laid out starkly in the official SEAL ethos. "We train for war and fight to win," each new SEAL is expected to affirm. "I stand ready to bring the full spectrum of combat power to bear in order to achieve my mission and the goals established by my country. The execution of my duties will be swift and violent when required yet guided by the very principles that I serve to defend." That last phrase sums things up very nicely, I think: "Swift and violent when required yet guided by the very principles that I serve to defend."

KILLING IS NECESSARY

Evil thrives only among the weak. In nature, predators don't have very many predators. Prey have predators. Cougars, bears, tigers—I don't remember seeing too many Discovery Channel episodes about *them* being victimized by other creatures of the wild. Nature is one long story of the strong preying on the weak.

That pattern holds in the human realm as well. The strong rarely get attacked. The savage or the evil almost always prefer to have their way with the weak and vulnerable. You see this almost anywhere human beings interact—from the ball field to the street corner to the executive suite. Street criminals don't look for strong, confident, resilient people to rob. They seek out the easiest victims. The young woman stopped alone at a traffic light. The drunk man weaving down the sidewalk. The older couple out for an evening stroll. That's who the bad guys target. They want easy marks. They're not seeking fair fights.

I hear people ask, "Why can't we all just get along?" or "Why can't the world just live in peace?" I just don't think we're designed as human beings for such a utopia to ever take hold. Maybe I'm just reflecting the gritty and violent war zones that have been part of my life for so long. But I suspect that if there were two people left on earth and only one chicken, they'd be fighting each other not just to avoid starvation, but also over who got to feast on the breast meat and who had to make do with a wing. So while it would be nice if the whole world lived in peace and harmony, I'm not holding my breath. Until that glorious day arrives, there will be predators, and there will be prey.

As a nation, we've found it necessary to kill for self-protection and the protection of the weak. The Revolutionary War. The Civil War. World War I. World War II. Korea. Vietnam. Afghanistan. Iraq. Lots of Americans would have said no to some of them. Hardly anyone would have said no to all of them, just like very few Americans are strict vegans who refuse to wear leather shoes or belts. We have had the experience in this country of seeing wars stop evil. The Civil War had huge costs for America, but would anyone argue that in stopping slavery it didn't have a valuable result? The death toll in World War II was staggering. But again, the Nazis had to be stopped, and they were.

There are lots of people in this country who don't believe in hunting, who believe that killing an animal is wrong, just like there are many people who don't believe in war. Unless you are an absolute vegan, when it comes to hunting, there's a good deal of hypocrisy in this. If you eat meat and you give a hunter a hard time, I think you're totally off your compass. All you've done is find a proxy, giving away the job of procuring that steak to someone else, who, chances are, you've never even met. The cow didn't just die of natural causes and then jump onto your plate. So it is with war. It's one thing to be against it. That's the easy, feel-good choice. Any decent, sensible person would prefer to avoid war. But at some point, a line is crossed, and war becomes rational and even necessary. Reasonable people can disagree where that line is. When our nation is threatened. When another nation is threatened. When human atrocities pass a certain point. Wherever the precise line is, there is a line.

I hope the United States makes the choice to carry on our long, proud tradition of being strong and believing that some things are worth fighting for. If you won't fight, if you're unwilling to make the effort and put yourself on the line—especially if people know you are unwilling to fight—you become a target immediately. Being unwilling to fight is just as bad as being incapable of fighting. That's not where any great nation should want to be.

ALWAYS KILL WITH RESPECT

Deciding that killing is necessary only begins the moral analysis that war—or other types of combat—should evoke. The question arises of how to treat the killing of an enemy. There are many parallels between hunting and war, and valuable lessons to be learned and shared from both.

I like to hunt. For me, being a hunter of elk, deer, and other big game has been a healthy counterpoint to my military job, and it isn't all about the killing. When you talk to nonhunters, this is sometimes hard for them to understand. But no one loves or appreciates the animal more than the hunter. As certain as the sun will rise in the east tomorrow, a hunter loves and respects an elk much more than someone who doesn't hunt. That's a guarantee. Hunters care more about the lives of those animals, the way they live, their perpetuation, care, habitat, and ability to thrive—and not just so they can go and kill them. Hunters understand the life cycle of an animal. They understand the rhythms and the behaviors. They get very much in tune with the animal.

Have you ever seen what happens when experienced hunters have taken down an animal? The hunters approach quietly. It's not a raucous celebration. There are rarely high fives, whoops, or hollers. It is usually a very reverent moment. Some primitive cultures even eat the heart of an elk or a buffalo as a sign of respect, believing this transfers some of the animal's nobility or power.

Even in America's culture, the hunter will often take a moment, perhaps even thank the animal, offering quiet appreciation for the food that's going to be put on the table.

That genuine feeling of respect is not what most hunting opponents would imagine. But it's real.

When it comes to the enemy, I can't help feeling exactly the same way. Even as I am convinced down to my very core that what has occurred on the battlefield was an appropriate and necessary kill, it is still a feeling loaded with respect. It doesn't matter if the enemy was part of a force or an ideology that wishes to destroy me and everything I hold dear. He was still a human being, doing something not so far from what I was doing out there. When taking someone's life, there is no avoiding the person's human nature. I am absolutely aware of his familial connections, the fact that he must have parents, children, siblings, and friends. I am killing my own species. I take that personally.

There are, of course, differences between killing an enemy combatant and hunting an animal. If you put your sights on any ungulate—including an elk or a deer—that animal shares nothing in common with you. There's no shared blood. There's no physical resemblance. We're totally different critters.

That's why hunting bear is a unique and, for some hunters, disturbing experience. I've hunted bear. That's as close as I've gotten outside of war to the sensation of killing a human being. A bear, because of its anatomy and the way it lives, feels much more personal in a hunt. So many of a bear's behaviors mirror human behaviors. Bears sleep when it's cold outside. They hunt like humans do. They fish. They're big, hairy, and strong. When I look at a bear, especially when the animal rises to its two hind legs, standing tall and erect, it's like facing off with a human.

My friend Steve Rinella hosts a TV show called *MeatEater.* He and I have been bear hunting together in the Alaska Range. In stomach-turning detail, Steve described to me what some hunters have experienced when they skin out a bear. They take the hide off, peeling the fur back. Suddenly they are staring at a critter whose muscular physique looks an awful lot like that of a linebacker in the NFL. It can be shocking. I understand that reaction.

We don't skin the enemy on the battlefield or eat him, but we certainly hunt him down. Even in the heat of battle, it's impossible to ignore the fact that you are putting down your own species. In times of war, people often try to dehumanize the enemy, ascribing characteristics to the other side that are foreign and inexplicable, suggesting that the enemy has a different appreciation for life or a different tolerance for death. That kind of talk can be soothing, I suppose. But it has always rung hollow to me. Face it. We're killing another human being. Yes, it can be uncomfortable. But that's the reality.

In short, killing is a profound act that should always be taken seriously and done respectfully. If that's true of game hunting, it should be doubly true in war. If we are going to kill, we must do so with a conscious understanding of what we are doing, of what it means to take another life.

KILLING SHOULD FEEL LIKE KILLING

That's one thing that's troubling about some of today's technologies. They separate us further and further from the human consequences of the act of killing. On one side, I am very much for us pushing the newest technology and embracing the many advanced systems that make our warfare more controllable, precise, and efficient. At the same time, it can also spare innocent lives. But those new weapons technologies also bring false comfort with the illusion that taking a life is somehow cleaner, tidier, and less deadly. It separates the warrior from the war. And that reeks of self-deception. How do we judge the impact of our actions? What effect are we having on local cultures? Even when we win the war in some technical way, are we ever going to command the peace?

In the military, we have something nicknamed "Kill-TV." You've seen it on YouTube or cable TV—the grainy, black-and-white videos taken from a missile, aircraft, or a drone, tracking the hit from targeting to impact. It's like a greatest-hit reel of carnage from above. Kill-TV is dramatic. It's thrilling in a way and technologically amazing. But it also reveals a disturbingly chilling way to kill. Highly removed. At a safe distance. Often operating from miles— sometimes thousands of miles—away.

These Kill-TV videos have been called war porn, but they aren't compiled just for the thrill of weapons buffs. They serve an actual training purpose. And provide a real-time glimpse of what killing is like today.

"Okay, look," a voice will say. "I've got seventeen military-aged males moving south from this target."

A voice on the ground will respond.

"That's not us."

"That's a good target. You can hit that target."

"Fire."

And they do.

As quickly, cleanly, and precisely as that, it's done. The targeted humans have been destroyed.

The tone of voice is revealing and fascinating.

Balanced. Muted. Unemotional. That doesn't mean these are callous people. They're just doing their jobs. They're staying focused, staying calm. It's controlled and professional. Dropping a bomb on a city or launching a drone is a completely different thing from killing the same number of people in a series of house-by-house assaults. One big difference is the scale.

War conducted through a computer screen isn't any less of a war—it just feels that way, and I don't think that's entirely a good thing. Human lives are not just points on a screen. Killing is fundamentally changed when it's a tech sitting in an Aeron chair in Houston or Tampa, sucking on a Slurpee and squinting at a monitor, flying a Predator or a Reaper drone, dropping bombs on active targets in a country on the other side of the globe. Killing could hardly be any more impersonal than that. Taking another's life isn't a video game. When you kill, there is a human being who used to be alive and isn't anymore. If you are going to be an honest warrior, you must face that fact. I understand the advantages of warfare at a distance, but there's also something missing there.

I led more than two hundred combat-assault operations in Iraq. We took quite a few casualties. Dozens of enemy combatants were killed. I was leading those operations. Though I was fully armed, I wasn't the one doing the most shooting. My guys were. Still, I was pulled into firefights. I killed people, sometimes at a close distance, more often somewhat farther away. But on two occasions, I was close enough to clearly see the faces of the people I killed. I could very much tell what they looked like. I held eye contact with them. In both instances, they were shooting at me as I was shooting at them.

They were trying to kill me, and I was trying to kill them.

The result was the one I hoped for. Obviously, I am thankful for the outcome.

There were many other times when I was shooting from three, four, or five hundred yards away, trading volleys with enemy combatants across a valley or up a hill. Did I hit someone? Did I not? Were they killed or merely wounded? Was there collateral damage involved? I don't know the answers to those questions. There was no safe way to inspect the results of those firefights, and I was too far away to see.

For many people at war, this is their only experience. Not knowing. Not sure. Never fully able to tell. Maybe they killed someone. Maybe they didn't. There is no way to know. There are no scoreboards on the battlefield.

Close-quarters combat is an entirely different experience. Kicking down a door, rushing inside a house, weapons raised from the moment of entry—that's as raw and rugged as battle can get.

You're inside a residence. Everyone is face-to-face. Inside, the people are so close you can smell them. Depending on exactly how close you are, the blood of the enemy can splatter back on your uniform. That's intimate and that's intense. But it's not indiscriminate. Often, we held our fire and no blood was shed. Maybe we searched the premises for bomb-making materials or an individual we were looking for. When it's a drone doing the job, on-the-ground assessments are no longer possible. The friendlies are all back at a safe distance. The armed eye in the sky is doing the work. That's the whole point of using drones.

It's the snipers, in my opinion, who in many ways have the most intense killing experience. Maybe it's a coin toss between them and an up-close, deadly-force encounter. Snipers often have the luxury of time, patiently following a target for minutes, even hours, waiting for the perfect shot. But the instruments of war employed by snipers bring them excruciatingly close to their target. Their scopes cut the distance. At one or two hundred yards away, using a very high-powered rifle scope, they are absolutely looking at the facial expressions and emotional reactions of their targets, getting to know them in that high-intensity period before the trigger pull.

Snipers see it in real time—they follow it from beginning to end. They squeeze the trigger. They watch the person fall. The sniper is the one who is making it happen. Life or death rests in his hands. This isn't a TV show. It isn't a video game. It's real. Do that a few dozen times—then tell me you don't have trouble falling asleep at night.

We put a tremendous weight and responsibility on the shoulders of our snipers. They know they need to get it right. To that end, they often work with a spotter, a person who's helping identify potential targets and also bearing some of the emotional weight of the potential kill.

"Red."

"Red."

"Red."

"Green."

That's the usual pattern. You're coming off safety. You're taking a couple of deep breaths. Align the sight. Control the trigger. Squeeze.

The round goes. You just took someone's life.

That experience, repeated over and over again, has to take an emotional toll.

Some people are affected very negatively and will suffer real psychological damage from the experience. Some are able to process and move on. It's a hard-to-define collision between the individual and the experience. It's what you did and who you are, and it's damn near impossible to separate the experience from the man. Of course, this is one of the risks of face-to-face combat, but I'd still rather make those judgments on the ground.

WE'RE BETTER THAN OUR ENEMIES

All special operators know our enemies. We fully grasp their savagery. We have seen what evil they are capable of. The current enemy we face truly wishes to usher in the Apocalypse.

These people are intent on spreading their violent repression around the world and destroying any force that opposes them. They seek to drag the entire planet back to the Dark Ages and obliterate the modern values of the West. With the help of digital social media—one product of modernity they embrace—they have demonstrated disturbing success recruiting young converts, many of whom are ready to kill innocents and give up their own lives for the cause. These are fighters as dedicated and ruthless as any the world has ever seen.

The names keep shifting. Al-Qaeda. ISIS. ISIL. The Islamic State. It'll be something else tomorrow. But the zealous impulse and the vicious tactics do not change fundamentally. They just keep getting worse. These are people who can burn a Jordanian pilot alive in a cage in the middle of the desert then broadcast the video on YouTube. To them, a televised beheading is no different from any other act of war. They'll just as soon kill a journalist or an aid worker as they will a competing warlord. They'll execute people in front of their families without a second thought. And from time to time, they will export their terror overseas, to London, Tel Aviv, Paris, Mumbai, Singapore, Jakarta, or New York.

The question for America and the West is what should we bring to a fight as tough as this one, a fight with an enemy so brutal and the stakes so high? Bring everything, I say.

I am by no means a warmonger. If I were commander

in chief, I would be the most reticent, circumspect leader our nation has had in a long time. War is horrible. I have seen it up close, and I know. I have seen too many of my SEAL brothers killed and wounded to think otherwise. I have seen too many disturbing civilian casualties. As commander in chief, I would exhaust every possible measure and opportunity to avoid war—diplomacy, negotiations, sanctions, and anything else I could possibly think of. I am all for avoiding war, until the moment finally comes when we have to fight one, and so we must. Then, if I were in charge, the fight with today's enemies would be one with only a single acceptable outcome: absolute, total destruction of our enemy—*absolute, total destruction.* I would call for whatever it took to prevail, including the full application of any and every weapon and tactic available. In war, there is no sense in fighting with half measures and a tiny fraction of our capacity. Otherwise, stay home.

The United States has an immense arsenal at its disposal: the most potent and high-tech weaponry and the best-trained special operators on earth, backed by a massive force of highly impressive conventional troops. When we go into battle, we should fight with everything we have. Then, when we're finished, we can offer an olive branch to help rebuild our enemy's nation, as we did so successfully with Germany and Japan after World War II.

We could defeat today's enemies swiftly if our nation could stomach the methods we would use. When we have been allowed, the Navy SEALs, Army Special Forces, Rangers, Air Force, and Marine Corps SOF have achieved tremendous success. We proved that in Iraq and Afghanistan, where SEAL and other special-operations units with boots on the ground and air support from above, could pulverize the enemy. But far too often, we were told not to use tactics we knew would work. The rules of engagement, drafted by lawyers at the Pentagon, held us back. We could have been so much more efficient than we were, our noble victories lasting far longer. To many who fought in Afghanistan and Iraq, it was truly maddening to have battle-zone tactical decisions made by lawyers and bureaucrats in Washington, and not by the commanders in the field and the troops on the ground.

If we had no rules of engagement, if tomorrow we were told we could go to the battlefield and do whatever we had to do—let the operators on the ground figure it out—we could defeat our enemies in short order. The goal of absolute destruction means that things would get ugly. I have no doubt about that. I'm talking about the worst parts of Old Testament justice, nothing subtle about those tactics. Using the same techniques our enemies use on *their* enemies. It would be disturbing, but it wouldn't last very long. And this is the language these people understand. Violence. Brute force. The absence of restraint and mercy. It is the language they speak among themselves. These are exactly the kinds of methods they have employed, their own chosen rules of engagement.

I'm not saying this is absolutely what we should be doing to fight the enemies we are facing right now. The American people are not ready to accept the level of violence required—yet. But as we search for a way to defeat an enemy that plays by no rules, we are sure to consider this in the not-so-distant future. It may come to that. As the American people and leaders come to understand what a self-imposed disadvantage we are operating under, as our enemies continue to establish their brutal hegemony across more of the Middle East, could we see a political resolve in America to bring more of our own arsenal to bear? It may take another attack on American soil, God forbid.

If and when our leaders are ready to attack the problem with whatever it takes to win, we already have the people on our teams who are capable of turning the tide in that part of the world very quickly. I have fought with some of them. They're highly trained warriors. They understand that, when they're sent into battle, their job is to dominate. Emotionally, they are prepared to do that job and be comfortable with its consequences. They would not be American special operators if this were not true.

WHEN KILLING BECOMES TOO MUCH

I feel very much in balance with the choices I have made. I also feel blessed because I feel I got the right amount of killing while defending our nation—the right amount for me, if such a concept isn't too grotesque. I didn't join the SEAL teams because I thought I'd get to work on a construction project. I could have joined the construction battalions or become a submarine driver or performed some other vital task in the military. If I just wanted to be in uniform and act as a fundamental part of the mission, there were lots of other things I could have done. "Meat eaters" is what the SEALs call other SEALs who have killed in battle. Until that happens, a special operator is still a newbie, living off expectations and things he's heard. Truthfully, I'd have been disappointed if I became a warrior and never experienced the fundamental act warriors perform. But I'm also grateful I didn't do too much of it to cross a threshold I wouldn't be comfortable with.

Warfare isn't a game. Killing someone isn't sinking a three-pointer just as the buzzer sounds. But killing is the ultimate experience of warfare, its very essence, and I'm even more grateful I wasn't on the receiving end.

Like many warriors and athletes, I have a script running silently through my head, a romanticized version of the high-cost life I have chosen that comes from Hannibal bringing the elephants to the battlefield and the samurai's notion of honor and respect, defeat and loss. It comes from a thousand stories I have heard since I was a boy. But it's there, and it's powerful, and it doesn't let go.

When a samurai was defeated on the battlefield, he would willingly take his own life, asking a second warrior to stand behind him and assist the suicide. It was costly, but that was their belief. They had a powerful notion of victory and completion, a very particular warrior code.

That code has always meant something to me. It resonated when my father read those stories to me and my younger brother at bedtime. I still have them rattling around in my head. They have informed my major decisions and followed me throughout my life. I carry them with me.

But I have buddies in some advanced SEAL teams that I can say with confidence have killed too much—too much for their own good. Their service to the nation is unimpeachable. I'm not saying that they didn't accomplish what they were asked to and then some, but killing as many people as they did has deeply affected a couple of my close friends.

These are guys I always knew as jokers and pranksters. They were quick with a funny comment and always lighthearted. I never hear them laughing now. I just don't get much of that from them anymore. These are strong, centered men. They are as clear as ever about what they have done and why they have done it. They certainly never seemed fragile in any way. But killing takes its toll on people, even strong people, and it's hard to know exactly where any individual's threshold lies.

Most healthy human beings have a limit. Those who aren't capable of feeling anything are sociopaths, and that's a bigger problem. These people are out there, including, no doubt, in the military, but they aren't the SEALs I'm talking about. These two guys are normal men asked to take on abnormal assignments that ultimately caught up with them.

I do believe we are all multiple versions of ourselves. When it comes to killing—doing the job I have signed up for and devoted a big slice of my life to—there are definitely two distinct men inside me. There is the man I am on a SEAL team and the man I am at home. I try to compartmentalize. I live parallel lives. I keep reminding myself how just the cause is. Put it like this: the man I am on the battlefield and the *gentleman* I am as a husband and father back here. Those are two different people. But here's the surprising part: they operate from the same moral compass. They share the same background foundations that guide and animate the behavior of both versions of me.

But still. The person who is willing to level sights on another human being and take a life is a different person from the one I am in daily life.

Thank God, I should add.

Every day in my years of active duty, I was in some kind of a fight. Some days, it was actual combat on the battlefield. Other days, the combat was in the form of a training exercise, where a buddy might be jumping on my back and trying to choke me while I tried to break free, spin around, and choke him. SEALs are very competitive animals.

Now, in my day-to-day life, I have stepped back from that. I am living in the civilian world, which has been fascinating to rediscover through SEAL eyes.

At some point, probably sooner rather than later, I'm going to see if my two daughters want to go fishing or hunting with me. Both those activities expose a child to death, even if it's just taking a trout out of the stream. It's a start, a beginning to understanding life and death. What's necessary, what's justifiable, what's acceptable. These conversations are going to happen. How could they not? They're central to who I am, pivotal to questions I'm sure the girls will have about their father. I don't have a timetable in my mind or a speech prepared. When the time comes, I'll just work through it the best way I can. I'll explain how I feel honestly. I respect the quarry. I respect the prey, especially when it's an animal that's going to provide us with food. We all have places in the world. We are interdependent.

When the conversation eventually moves along to killing another person, I will try to explain that reality as well.

TRIDENT TAKEAWAYS

- Be the hunter, not the hunted.
- Kill with respect.
- Even meat eaters can get too full.

CHAPTER 5

LEADERSHIP SECRETS OF THE SEALS

Coming up as a SEAL officer, I had the excellent fortune to be exposed to many officers I admired. Watching them, I learned that there is no handy checklist for world-class leaders. Some of it is instinct. Some of it is force of personality. Some of it entails surrounding yourself with the right foot soldiers and peers—people who share your vision and are also energetic, creative, and trustworthy. And a large part of it—maybe the most significant part—requires thinking strategically about the impact you are having on the people you aspire to lead. That key relationship, whether in military or civilian life, gets far less careful attention than it deserves. In large and small ways, it tips the balance between failed and successful leadership.

All great leaders bring their own personalities to the job,

which is why there are great charismatic leaders, great intellectual leaders, great moral leaders, and great leaders who seem to have little personality at all. But learn the can't-miss leadership qualities that I lay out here, and you will be very much on your way.

LEADERS MAKE THE DECISIONS, SHOULDER THE BURDENS, AND LIVE WITH THE RESULTS

Consensus is a very popular concept now. It sounds inclusive, broadly respectful, and personally decent. Far too often, it is an excuse for weak leadership. Leaders, listen up. You get paid to lead. You're in the driver's seat now. A real leader stands up and takes charge.

There is a reason Margaret Thatcher, British prime minister, was known as "the Iron Lady," and it was usually meant as a compliment. She had a short list of world-changing ambitions and a disdainful definition for consensus: "The process of abandoning all beliefs, principles, values, and policies in search of something in which no one believes, but to which no one objects; the process of avoiding the very issues that have to be solved, merely because you cannot get agreement on the way ahead. What great cause would have been fought and won under the banner: 'I stand for consensus'?"

Iron, indeed.

My personal style of decision-making is to begin with some key ideas, solicit input early, incorporate the feedback I receive, and then finalize a plan. That plan is the plan that gets executed.

On my team, the men understood this rhythm. There generally were just a few guys involved at the start. The chief, my leading petty officer, a couple of other key guys who had proven themselves to be talented planners, and I pulled together the mission details. This part couldn't be done by committee, at least not a very large one. Still, everyone had a role to play in whatever the ultimate plan was going to be. So while a select few were strategizing, the other guys were getting the gun trucks ready, making sure we had enough ammo, and checking that their gear was tight.

Then it was time to brief and finally rehearse the mission. Up through rehearsals, all opinions were welcome. I wanted feedback—in fact, I demanded it. It could save lives. At that point, anyone from the most junior guy up was free to say, "I don't think it's smart to use ladders going over those fences. There's a three-story building over here. We could be compromised. I think we should crash through the front gate or sneak in the back side." Rank didn't matter. Job responsibilities didn't apply. If someone had something to contribute, I wanted it laid right out there. I wanted my men to make suggestions, express reservations, whatever it was. That was my expectation of my team—all insights were valued.

With the input of my men, the team would move into the final rehearsals. When we completed those rehearsals, I'd still be open to any last-minute observational suggestions.

Typically, once I felt that everyone knew what we were doing and everyone understood the plan, the time to talk it out as a team was over. We were a team. Everyone had participated. Still, I was in charge, and the decisions had been made. Every man on my team understood what that meant. As soon as night fell, we'd hop in the trucks to begin executing our mission. We'd start our drive to the target. While we were on the road—while we were on the road!—if any one of my guys decided to pop on the radio and say, "I have a good idea. Maybe we should use those ladders, after all," I would chop their heads off. My team knew I would absolutely lose my mind. Our time for planning was long done. When it was time to go to work, we were going with the plan.

CERTAIN ISN'T THE SAME AS RIGHT

Of course, sticking stubbornly to your own opinion is a sure way to make unnecessary mistakes. One of my very first mentors and a widely respected SEAL learned this one the hard way.

We were in the rolling hills of Fort Knox, Kentucky, a beautiful part of the country dotted with gullies, fast-flowing rivers, and steep ravines. At one point, we had finished a patrol exercise, where the instructors were evaluating a group of us. The group, including the instructor, got lost. Not lost in a dangerous way, but we didn't know exactly where we were. It was pitch-black outside and we were using night vision. Were our trucks up this hill—or that hill? We didn't have a clue.

The lead instructor was trying to walk us out of there. Brian was walking behind him, and I could see he was getting enraged.

"I'm not sure, I'm not sure," I could hear the instructor saying.

"Screw this," Brian said with equal measures of frustration and bravado. "Follow me." Exactly what a leader should say.

But he took a step to the right and fell thirty feet down a ravine. It could have been far worse. Luckily, he didn't hurt himself too badly. But it was a tumbling, rolling mess.

I will never forget that "follow me."

The lead instructor looked down into the darkness where Brian had disappeared and said softly, almost under his breath, "Do we have to?"

A heroic leader shouldn't be inflexible. Leadership does sometimes require being prepared for change midstream. When we got to the mission location, if circumstances were different from what we expected and the plan had to be altered, no problem. Flexibility is a key talent on the modern battlefield. SEALs have a reputation for creativity, and it is well deserved.

With a lot of leaders there's hemming and hawing, going back and forth, making decisions, and then flipping them upside down based on the latest comment or criticism any member of the team makes. That's where I've seen a lot of ineffective leaders doing a poor job.

Building internal support is good and necessary. That does not mean slavishly seeking consensus. There is an admiral I worked with who liked to invite everyone to the table for endless discussions. These meetings were always entertaining and they often went on for hours. Every single person was heard. And they all left happy, convinced their own particular positions had won the day.

"I don't think it works like that, sir," I tried to warn the admiral after one of his famous get-togethers. "Six people should be upset right now, and one person is supposed to be happy with you—just one. You've got everybody thinking they are about to get the big prize."

I knew—and on some level, he must have known—that such a result wasn't possible. Soon enough, the others would figure it out as well. Then he'd have seven people who weren't just upset they hadn't gotten what they'd hoped for. They'd be angry that they'd been misled. And they wouldn't trust him the next time.

If you want to guarantee failure as a leader, try achieving universal agreement on almost anything. If you can get most of your people on the same page, consider yourself lucky, and press ahead. Sometimes you need to press ahead even if you can't. In general, to get significant things accomplished, you have to be willing to crush a few souls.

Get used to it: no strong leader is one hundred percent loved. Holding out for that will lower your likability score to zero percent loved and will also lower your effectiveness. Any leader who gets important things done will inevitably upset some of the people beneath, beside, and above him. The lazy. The self-protective. The change resistant. The people who had a cushy deal with previous leadership and don't want to upset that arrangement. Those people are supposed to resent you. The fact that they do is a good sign. If you can't point to a few people in that category, chances are your performance as a leader isn't strong enough.

If you're a real leader, 80 to 90 percent of the people you work with will like the decisions you are making, be on board with what you're doing, and say you are the type of leader they want to be around. That's a pretty good ratio. The rest will loathe, resent, and absolutely despise you and what you stand for. They'll be convinced you're the biggest nightmare that has ever swept into their lives. If you don't have those people, you don't stand for anything. You don't hold the line for the things that matter. If everybody thinks you're great, that's a problem.

"You have enemies? Good," Winston Churchill said. "That means you've stood up for something, sometime in your life."

Damn right. Leaders have to possess the intestinal fortitude to make the tough decisions. Leaders also have to accept responsibility for the choices they make.

I believe I have read every major speech Abraham Lincoln delivered. In all those speeches, I never once remember him saying, "It's James Buchanan's fault."

General George Patton was unequivocal about this: "Do not make excuses, whether it's your fault or not."

But Benjamin Franklin said it even better: "He that is good for making excuses is seldom good for anything else."

It's a lesson today's leaders need to embrace. When will they shed the past and deal with the now? Leading is not primarily about cleaning up the mess you inherited. It's about moving forward to create something better. To hell with who screwed it up behind you. We see this in politics. We see it in business. We see it in the military. No one sees strength in the person who complains about the person who messed everything up before you.

I've noticed corporate America has become somewhat less tolerant of the kinds of excuses many politicians use. More frequently today, the board of directors will tell a new CEO,

"Yes, the last guy was a disaster. Either make it right or you'll be tossed out of here the same way he was."

Sadly, that message has yet to filter its way through to our top elected leaders. From county government to state legislatures to Washington, making excuses has never been more popular than it is today. Both sides seem to waste an awful lot of time and energy trying to pin responsibility on those who came before.

It wasn't always this way. There has always been partisanship, but at least people talked a better game. As President John Kennedy famously said: "Let us not seek the Republican answer or the Democratic answer, but the right answer. Let us not seek to fix the blame for the past. Let us accept our own responsibility for the future." And people actually took him seriously.

It sounds like a million years ago, doesn't it? Now it's almost always someone else's fault. That's blame-casting—not leadership.

LEADERS SET ACHIEVABLE GOALS— THEN ACHIEVE THEM

One of the first lessons we teach SEAL snipers is "narrow the focus." Being an effective sniper takes a whole lot more than aiming a rifle, peering through a scope, and pulling the trigger. Weapon selection, environmental conditions, stealth-and-concealment—all those factors figure in.

Before you can hit a target, you have to find the target, and sometimes that's the most challenging part. Narrow the field of vision. That's the very first step. When you concentrate your field of view, you end up seeing more. That's how you find things: look at less. It's counterintuitive, I know. It's also true.

If you're staring at a massive hillside in Afghanistan, sweeping left and right with a pair of field binoculars, chances are you won't see much of anything. Soon enough, you'll be asking yourself or your buddies: "Weren't there supposed to be enemy combatants out there?" It's the same thing hunters discover gazing across a broad forest for elk, bear, or deer. All they see at first is a blur of greens and browns.

But sector off that giant hillside. Divide the terrain into a mental grid. Build the flanks and concentrate. Suddenly your focus will sharpen. Tiny movements will be easier to spot. Inside those narrow confines, an intricate pattern will reveal itself. That's one way our snipers find the bad guys to take out.

You will hear versions of "narrow the focus" all over the SEAL community—from the strategies we follow to the rucks we carry into battle. In the military, that's what we call a backpack, a ruck. I still remember the first ruck I was issued when I arrived at SEAL Team Four. It was an Army Alice, a medium-size green canvas model that American soldiers have been carrying for decades. It isn't much to look at, but it's rugged, snug, and reliable. You can pack a lot of weight in one of those things. In fact, you can stuff more weight in there than most people can comfortably carry. Don't do that. You will regret it.

One of my guys was an avid mountaineer. He bought a massive, off-the-shelf backpack from Dana Design, a high-end pack builder based in the Rocky Mountains. Everybody loved the look of this beautiful backpack. Solid straps, a soft waistband, redundant zippers, and straps designed so that even if one of them failed, the contents of the ruck would still be safe. I slid the pack on empty. It was perfect. But everyone forgot the First Rule of Ruck: no matter how large or small your ruck is, you are going to fill it up.

This might sound familiar from family vacations. Whether you take a small carry-on or a huge steamer trunk, you will fill it to the brim, and every single item you throw in there will seem totally necessary.

You can guess what happened with my mountaineering team member and his beautiful Dana Design ruck. He filled that sucker with so much clothing and gear, the first time he took it out on a mission, he ended up leaving it behind in one of the trucks. The ruck was a thing of beauty, but far too heavy to carry for more than a few hundred yards. Luckily, we had an extra Army Alice aboard. He was able to make do perfectly well with that—and half the gear he'd come with.

As it is with snipers and rucks, so it is with leaders today. If you intend to be an effective leader, you need to learn to narrow your field of vision and be careful about what you pack in your ruck. Metaphorically speaking, of course. You should certainly ask yourself: "Am I doing a good job spotting my targets? How large a load can I carry?"

I am often surprised at all the things our nation's leaders believe they can accomplish. Not how large the objectives are—but how many they hope to achieve. Programs to launch. Nations to build. Constituencies to placate. Inequities to cure. Cultures to improve.

I suppose in a way this is admirable—having a lengthy agenda and busily pursuing every last item on it. I admit, it's better than having no agenda at all. And maybe I'd feel differently if I looked at the long list of things our leaders promised to accomplish and saw an equally long column of check marks.

Instead, what we've been getting are endless rows of *incompletes*. Good intentions, diligent efforts, ever-delayed deadlines, sighs of disappointment. Whatever the particular promise—rising middle-class wages, deeper respect abroad, improved student test scores, fewer crumbling roads, a competitive workforce, immigration reform, peace in this or that nation, freer and fairer trade—we hear the same thing over and over again: "We tried. We'll try again next year."

Wouldn't it be better to win one war than to dabble in half a dozen? Wouldn't it be better to solve one major social problem than to fail at solving ten? Narrow the field of vision. Keep your ruck light.

I understand that American presidents don't have the luxury of tending to only one issue at a time. A nation as large and diverse as ours has many needs. But by now, this scattershot approach is starting to feel almost irresponsible. Everything is thrown at the wall and nothing is sticking. At some point, giving it a good try just isn't enough.

It's long past the time when our top leaders need to stop worrying about how popular they are, collect themselves, and say: "I'm not going to try to solve everything." Or even better: "I'm going to try to solve three problems in the next four years, and failure is not an option on any of these." Three not thirty. That way, at least our country has a good chance of ending up with three problems off the table.

When I was in my last command—the number two position—we got a new commanding officer. He was an energetic leader and a respected buddy of mine, someone whose dedication and commitment I admire. We'd made some good progress before he arrived, and I'd drawn up a list for him of all the unfinished business we had. He looked at my stack of major issues, reading it carefully. Then he asked me: "How many of these things do you think we can get done?"

I gave him my best advice. "If you pick your top issue and maybe one more and we go all in, you and I and the whole command working for it, we might get them across the line in the two years you are going to be here. If you try for too much, you're going to pass this exact same deck of issues on to the next commander." In his *Principles of War*, the Prussian military strategist Carl von Clausewitz embraced this clearly. "Pursue one great decisive aim with force and determination," he urged.

My commanding officer said he agreed. But then he started ticking off all the important items he wanted to accomplish. There were a lot of them, and they all sounded legitimate. "They need doing," he said. I couldn't disagree with that part. "I think we should probably try," he said.

He ended up identifying eight major issues and eventually gave some attention to dozens of smaller ones as well. The only notable change we made in those two years—the only one—was that we got a brand-new blue awning built outside of the stairway that led up to the main office of the command.

The awning wasn't even one of the original eight tasks. And while it was a nice awning—I can't deny that—it wasn't much to show for two years of effort. By the time he left, we had eight major issues still on the to-do list and a couple of new ones that had popped up during those two years.

A leader who sets authentic goals achieves more than the leader who unrealistically shoots for the stars.

LEADERS DON'T LET EGO GET IN THE WAY

The higher you go up the chain of command, the more elevation to your title in the C-Suite, the more people you are in service to. However many people it is, they are now your responsibility. Some people think just the opposite is true. They are convinced being higher up the flagpole means there are more people who now work for them. Believe that and you are blind to what defines a good and respected leader.

My dad started in a law firm the same year I was born. He was especially close with one of the founding partners, John Appel. When my brother and I were little, we used to ride horses and go shooting on Mr. Appel's ranch. He was the first leader I ever noticed, and I still remember a leadership lesson I learned from him.

One morning, my father was in his office, racing to prepare for a court hearing when Mr. Appel stuck his head in. "Anything going on?" he asked.

My father explained quickly that he was preparing for

court but was short one important argument that a paralegal could help write up. He asked if Mr. Appel would have her do it as soon as she came in.

"Sure," the senior partner said as my dad hustled out the door.

Half an hour later, Dad was sitting at the front of the courtroom waiting for the judge to come, when a hand reached over the railing holding a two-page memo. My dad looked up to see Mr. Appel. The memo was right on point, cleanly written with case cites and everything. The senior partner hadn't waited for the paralegal to draft the argument or for the firm messenger to rush it over to court. He'd done it himself.

I remember my dad telling that story years later. "There is no job too small for a leader," he said.

Much of leadership isn't large, sweeping actions. It's about setting values in an organization and convincing other people to share them. Don't make excuses. Lead by example. Don't ask others to do anything you wouldn't do yourself. These are commonsense practices, but it's amazing how often people in leadership positions seem to forget them.

As a leader, no necessary task should be beneath you. This includes making the coffee, cleaning the toilets, taking out the trash. If you're too good to do those things, suck it up and pretend you aren't. Otherwise, you'll never gain the respect of the people you aspire to lead. Do you have any idea how many points can be scored with skeptical subordinates from a small, humble act? Try taking a phone message, offering to share a donut, or issuing the tiniest compliment. You'll see. Once you grasp that, you'll be doing nice things for others every day. But don't worry, the leader who is too full of himself to understand the power of humility will almost certainly have the realization forced on him—or he won't be a leader for long.

On the SEAL teams, the guys can always tell the difference between the leader who lets his ego get in the way and one who understands that no job is too small for him. They know the officers who are willing to pack their own bags, drive their own vehicles, and perform other menial tasks. If you are the kind of officer who needs to be pampered, don't be surprised if you're soon hearing what I call the "sarcastic sir."

"Let me get that for you, *sir*"—only the "sir" won't be a sign of respect anymore. It'll sound more like a taunt or a sneer.

Message delivered, message received.

Once your team sees that you don't think you're too good to do the less glamorous work, they'll respect you more. They'll work harder for you. They'll feel more invested in the goals you set. And they'll happily carry your bags.

LEADERS THINK STRATEGICALLY ABOUT THE IMPACT THEY'RE HAVING ON THOSE THEY ASPIRE TO LEAD

Ultimately, a leader can't force people to follow. He has to inspire. I had an officer at the basic-training command who didn't have any idea how he came across. He was a super-bright guy. But he was a classic case of book-smart, not people-smart. He didn't realize how people perceived him or how his less-than-endearing manner impacted those around him. What was his difficulty relating to the people who worked below him? He was one of those men who was so brilliant he was constantly frustrated that others didn't have the same brainpower.

He had certainly impressed those above him. It wasn't unusual to hear his higher-ups say, "He's a rising superstar. He's moving forward and becoming a senior leader." But if you asked any person below him, even someone who was a single rank below him, they'd say, "He's the biggest galactic disaster I've ever been around . . . I wouldn't follow that guy anywhere."

And the subordinates were right. He never reached the heights he was capable of. Respect has to flow up *and* down.

John Schofield, who fought in the Civil War and later served as U.S. secretary of war, put it like this: "The one mode or the other in dealing with subordinates springs from a corresponding spirit in the breast of the commander. He who feels the respect which is due to others cannot fail to inspire in them respect for himself; while he who feels, and hence manifests, disrespect toward others, especially his subordinates, cannot fail to inspire hatred against himself." Or as one of my teammates grumbled about our basic-training officer: "He kisses every butt to the north and treats everyone to the south like garbage."

Respecting your troops means taking care of what they need. Sometimes, a leader has to be willing to fight for those he leads. You should do this sincerely, but sometimes a bit of showmanship helps. I wasn't above laying it on a little thick to the senior leadership when I went to bat on behalf of my guys. "We've got to fight for the boys on this one," I'd say.

It could be something large or small—maybe my guys want to be able to leave a half hour early or we've been working for four weeks straight and need a couple nights off. It's usually small things, but oftentimes it's the small things that are the biggest things in the moment. Fighting for those nights was a big deal to my men, and it meant something to them to see me fight for them.

Some of the leadership above me would deny my request, which could have been the end of the discussion. In the military, when rank comes into play, it often is. But not always.

"Bull!" I'd say. "My guys are not coming in tomorrow. I'll stay. I'll be here. But my guys won't be here."

"Hell, yeah," the guys say. "LT is fighting for us."

Demonstrate you're a leader who cares about what your team needs. Sometimes, with odds that are seriously stacked against you, you'll win. And sometimes you've got to recognize when your luck fails and you've got to follow orders. Knowing you fought for them, your team will jump into the fight with that much more vigor and respect. This is how a true leader can become a hero in the eyes of his men.

LEADERS KNOW THE VALUE OF KEEPING THE TROOPS OFF BALANCE, AT LEAST A LITTLE

Leaders with a known leadership rhythm can sometimes surprise—often, it can be the off-the-battlefield gestures that leave a lasting impression. I don't drink or smoke cigarettes. But occasionally I enjoy a cigar. It throws people off who know me when they see me once in a while appreciating a cigar. I like that little bit of unpredictability. It's such a small thing, but it keeps people guessing. On some level, it makes them wonder what else they don't know about me and how else I might catch them off guard.

As a leader, being predictable and dependable are important traits. But it's also good to take people by surprise sometimes and leave them a little off balance. And little is key here. Small things that are somewhat unexpected get just the right amount of notice, just enough to make folks pay attention. A little jolt creates energy and acts as a counterbalance to laziness and lethargy.

When it comes to being predictable, 90 percent of the time is a good number to shoot for. Be 90 percent predictable, but 10 percent of the time catch people unawares. Nothing too drastic. You don't want people thinking you're actually unbalanced. But do something unexpected and push yourself a little further than anyone expects. It'll have people believing they don't have you entirely figured out. That possibility of surprise is always lingering below the surface; no one knows when it might pop up.

And if they don't quite know what to expect—well, at least they'll be listening more carefully to you.

NEXT CHALLENGE: POLITICAL LEADERS

So what's the problem in Washington? Our leaders there seem unable to get much done, including many things almost everyone agrees are extremely important. Does anyone actually think the world is growing more peaceful? Do we truly believe the middle class is making progress? Are we convinced our immigration system is working as intended? Does anyone claim our kids are well prepared to compete globally? Does anyone contend that our health-care system is keeping us as healthy as it could? No, no, no, no, and no. Even more telling is that no one expects any of these issues to be solved anytime soon.

This is an inexcusable state for this country to be in given where we started. We didn't get to be the world's only superpower and most admired nation by weak leadership. We were guided to greatness by some extraordinarily effective leaders who knew what they wanted to achieve.

Our Founding Fathers were scholars, inventors, writers, and statesmen. They were successful businessmen and true intellectuals. Many of them achieved in a wide variety of disciplines. And we've had some towering national leaders in the two-plus centuries since then, leaders who were capable of extraordinary vision and huge achievement at home and abroad. Gaining freedom from the British. Settling the middle states and the west. Ending slavery and reuniting the nation after a bloody Civil War. Ending the Great Depression. Winning World War II. Creating a modern industrial economy, and then a modern technological one. Ending the Cold War and sending waves of freedom across Eastern Europe and the Soviet empire.

These were not the small achievements of hesitant men. And those leaders shared many of the same traits: they weren't dissuaded by a constant need for approval. Every one of their achievements required bold thinking, clear prioritizing, and a willingness to take the heat. They worked hard, without regard to status or job title. They inspired others.

Compare the diverse backgrounds of our nation's early leaders to the routes most modern presidents followed to the White House. Some of our recent presidents had excellent leadership qualities, but there was an undeniable sameness to their climbs. In reverse chronological order, here are the previous occupations of the last six: politician (senator), politician (governor), politician (governor), politician (vice president), politician (governor), and politician (vice president). Notice a pattern? We have to go back to the 1950s and General Dwight Eisenhower to find a U.S. president who didn't climb a traditional ladder of elective office into the White House.

Should incremental political ambition be the only route to the top? It's not a natural breeding ground for bold, focused leadership or creative problem solving. Today we need people who not only want to serve but who have the personality and intellect to lead effectively.

We have tremendous talent in this country. There's a reason the best of our companies in America are booming. They have great leaders. We have people—and this is not hyperbole—who have revolutionized the world. And we should try to duplicate some of that magic outside the product lab and the boardroom. Imagine if we drafted the top five people at Google, Amazon, and Uber and said to them: "Give us three years. Take what you have learned building these extraordinary companies and make America better. Solve problems. Envision opportunities. Improve things. Three years should be enough to make substantial progress." I'd keep it as open-ended as possible. Let them go where their instincts send them.

I can't tell you exactly what would come out of an experiment like that, but I bet it wouldn't look like business as usual in Washington. Business as usual isn't how Bill Gates built Microsoft, Warren Buffett launched Berkshire, or Steve Jobs guided Apple. Mediocrity and paralysis should not be the hallmarks of Washington.

Whatever the realm—the battlefield, the boardroom, or the capital—there are many different ways to lead. But all of them require leaders who are thoughtful, strategic, and willing to accept personal responsibility for their decisions—for the failures and successes alike.

TRIDENT TAKEAWAYS

- Leaders have a plan and execute it.
- Leaders build support for themselves and their ideas.
- Leaders never hold themselves above those they lead.

CHAPTER 6

WHY WE FIGHT

If you go into the military, especially if you are serving in a combat unit, this should come as no surprise: you will be asked to do a job, and that job may well involve the ultimate interaction between two human beings. You are trying to kill the enemy while the enemy is trying to kill you. That truly is the essence of warfare.

So the question arises: Why would any sane person want to volunteer for that? To me, some things are unquestionably worth dying for. The first thing I would die for—my family—hardly needs any explanation. If anyone threatened my bride, children, parents, brother, or my other close relatives—I'd put my close friends in this category—I would be the fiercest warrior imaginable.

I feel no equivocation about this, no lack of clarity, no

need to analyze how I feel. If anyone threatened my family, I would do whatever it took, including immediately risking my own life, to defend the people I love the most. To be honest, there is nothing I wouldn't do. And I'm pretty confident I would win. I have not a scintilla of doubt about any of this.

When I say that I would die for my country, I know that requires a greater explanation. What exactly do I mean? I can only speak to what it's like to wear the uniform of the United States of America. But to put on the colors of my country and protect the ideals that America stands for—that's always felt sacred to me. It gives meaning to an enterprise that, otherwise, no rational person would choose to engage in. Risking your own death. Inflicting death on others. Traveling great distances and enduring hardship for the chance to take that on. I can think of very few motivations that are powerful enough to convince someone to absorb all that.

The ancient Chinese philosopher Mencius laid it out with perfect clarity: "I dislike death," he said. "However, there are some things I dislike more than death. Therefore, there are times when I will not avoid danger." An attack on what this nation stands for and has to offer and on the great people who live here—to me—that's certainly worth dying for.

WE FIGHT TO PROTECT AMERICAN IDEALS

Look at all we have in this country worth fighting for. The great opportunities we are given. The liberty to run our own lives. The diversity. The decency. The natural beauty. I don't mean to sound like the Tourist Board or the Chamber of Commerce or the slogans on an Uncle Sam military recruiting poster, but there are many reasons why I love America and would risk my life to protect it.

I sincerely believe our country allows us to enjoy the very best that the world has to offer. I'm not talking about the modern conveniences and indulgences we have. Many nations have those today. I've been very lucky to travel the world. I love to experience other lands and cultures. But the truth is, there's not a thing in the world I couldn't find inside our country's borders if I never left again. I'll linger on just a few of the ways we are particularly blessed as Americans yet we rarely pause to recognize.

This piece of real estate called America is mind-boggling. On this broad continent from east coast to west coast, we have the mountains, deserts, valleys, oceans, rivers, lakes, prairies, and dense forests. If you want a tropical rain forest, we have Hawaii. We also have teeming cities, including several of the world's greatest: New York in the east, Chicago to the north, Dallas to the south, and San Francisco to the west. Spread out between our two perfect oceans—I say "our" because I'm in the Navy—we have some beautifully isolated expanses of fertile farmland.

We have friends to the north and south, even if we occasionally express frustration with them. Not many nations are as comfortable with their neighbors. Mexico and Canada aren't attacking us, and I don't expect them to anytime soon.

Our blessings don't stop with amazing geography. We all have the unique ability as citizens to improve our stations in life and know that something even better may be available to the next generation. Our long history of immigration and inclusion, openness to all faiths, and an endless variety of ideas means there are very few languages, cultures, or attitudes that cannot be experienced in America. We all have our own American Dream and a different American experience. I believe this is a huge part of our strength—the lack of enforced uniformity.

Truly, it is the idea of America, the values of America, the role that America represents for good in the world—that is what being an American means to me and what I would risk my life to defend. This has little to do with the identity of the commander in chief or the nation's current foreign policy, or even the strategic wisdom of the particular wars we might be fighting today.

In Iraq, most of my fellow SEALs were just interested in

doing the job. It's a common mind-set: "You could have sent me to Africa. You could have sent me to Yemen. It wouldn't have mattered. Wherever we're fighting, we're fighting. Just give me my job." Colonels and generals—they were weighing strategy. What the senior leadership and the politicians were doing back home, that was on another level entirely. What the boys were interested in was the best position to place effective fire, the best way to approach a target, and the most advantageous time to advance. When the talk turned to those issues, let me tell you, their eyes lit up, and they could make comparative assessments for the rest of the night.

When I arrived in Iraq, I had different thoughts in my head. I remembered the stories my father read to my brother and me when we were boys. Through those stories, I had learned that Alexander and his Macedonians had walked the same terrain I was now fighting on. That was powerful to me. They came marching right through this same land, then ended up in India, and marched back. I was aware of what it meant to be in the Euphrates River Valley, where so much history lived. This gave me a different perspective.

When I'd share those stories with my men, some of them would roll their eyes. "LT's history," they would say, chuckling, while generously bearing another one of my tedious monologues.

But to all of us risking our lives on that battlefield, our

commitment to America went much deeper than any single agency, policy, or politician. It had little to do with geo-politics. Little to do with the pieces on some global-power chessboard. Yes, those issues were all-important. I had my opinions about them, as did many of my fellow SEALs. But as warriors, none of that was truly our concern. That's not why we were fighting—or why we were fighting as one dedi-cated team.

For me and for most warriors, the inner dialogue is relatively straightforward: "My country needs me? Then I am there." It comes from a place of deep gratitude and respect. We are committed to the America we love and to the people who make up this amazing country.

WE FIGHT TO TEST OURSELVES

Obviously, the folks who seek to join the military, particu-larly the SEAL teams and other special-operations forces, know what risks they are signing up for. My early SEAL days were pre-9/11. I began my SEAL career before our nation was in a time of constant military conflict. In those halcyon days, being a SEAL was more like being a part of a cool, secret society—excellent friends, dangerous toys, seemingly endless time, money for exotic training exercises, and no enemies shooting back at us. What could be more fun than that? There's an aspect of this soldier's calling that is truly selfish, something that no honest warrior can ever fully deny. There's an ultimate-game component to a raging firefight that can't be matched in any other field.

Still, being a SEAL wasn't a risk-free enterprise even when America wasn't at war. We lost a guy a year, sometimes two guys a year, in training accidents—a free-fall mishap during jump evolutions or the occasional vehicle crash. I don't recall any fatal drownings, but I know the SEAL teams have suffered those tragedies over the years.

Given how intensely SEALs trained getting to the spot we felt necessary, those deaths were inevitable, we told ourselves. "We break some eggs" was the expression people used back then.

On some conscious level, though, most of us who join special forces are hoping for that wartime opportunity. Not hoping, certainly, for the opportunity to die. But all of us have struggled mightily, training in ways that pushed us to the breaking point. We prepared until we were fully ready to enter the fight and test ourselves where the possibility of death was clear and unavoidable. I know that's real. I've felt that desire.

Brain surgeons feel it. So do homicide detectives, forensic psychologists, NASCAR drivers, and EMTs. It's the special rush of being where life and death collide. The resulting adrenaline is far more motivating than a hefty paycheck. It's as addictive as crack cocaine. It's hard to explain in a way that doesn't make you sound bloodthirsty or callous, but I still don't believe that either of those characteristics often apply to true warriors.

The blood sport of war goes all the way back to the first two hungry cavemen facing off over a mastodon carcass.

"It's mine!"

"It's mine!"

Crack! "You die!"

The technology has changed over the millennia, as have the strategies, tactics, and destructive power of the weaponry. But the essential relationship between the two combatants is exactly the same as it's always been. The two of you confront each other in the most elemental and personal way: you with your teammates and armaments, he with his. The stakes are enormously high. Who lives? Who dies? Who kills whom? Those are the questions that matter.

To compete at a level where the risks are tolerable, you have to be all in, just as top athletes are in their sports, but even more so. Athletes are trained to leave it all on the playing field. I understand the intensity and drive of playing a sport to your fullest ability. But no one plays for stakes any larger than those on the battlefield. That is part of what pulled me in—the SEALs have an inner cohesion and a personal bond with one another that is stronger than any team I'd ever been part of before, and I'd been part of a few.

The wars that came after the terror attacks on New York, Washington, and Pennsylvania truly did change everything. Suddenly America was taking the fight to our enemies. My guys and I were at the tip of the spear.

Even when we went into Iraq and Afghanistan, not everyone in uniform faced the risks that the SEALs and other combat units did. Armies are complex organizations. They inevitably include many personnel who have about as much chance of dying on the job as junior-college professors or bank CEOs. Harm's way is not their way.

Warriors who are at the greatest risk of dying hardly think about death at all. They are busy training, busy strategizing, and, in some unfortunate cases, busy trying to avoid the risks. One of the first lessons we teach our new SEALs when they are learning gunfighting is "You gotta win the gunfight first. Then move on to whatever comes next." If your best friend is killed beside you, that's not the time to lament or mourn your fellow soldier. Keep focused and press on. It isn't easy, but sometimes a warrior needs to compartmentalize. We have to detach and realize, "My best buddy was just killed right next to me. We still need to win this fight or none of us are going home."

When it comes to death and warriors, repression is the order of the day. That, right there, is our own personal no-go zone. We don't dwell on the possibility of dying because doing so would be distracting to our purpose. It might undermine our drive and confidence. Focusing too much on the most dire of possibilities—I'm sorry, but that just gets in the way. If and when we do, we rarely admit it to one another. We don't even like to admit it to ourselves.

That's not to deny the obvious. People die in service. Frequently. And this is not an abstract generalization. On the SEAL teams, to a greater or lesser extent, death is always nearby. Serving requires accepting the presence of danger. When I talk to young SEAL candidates during training, the possibility of death is one of the harsh realities I always share with them. "I can't point to any one of you and say, 'You will die.' I can't point to someone else and say, 'You will live.' What I can assure you, given where you are sitting now, is some of your friends will die. Look around. Remember these faces. People you care about are going to die."

That goes for all of us warriors. The possibility is real every time I strap on my gear and head out on a mission. Combat is a risk-filled enterprise, especially for people like Navy SEALs who tend to do a lot of it in very dangerous places. Time and again, we are thrust into the most aggressive and highly charged encounters—bullets flying, bombs going off, a well-trained and highly motivated enemy on the other side. On the missions I led in Iraq, every single one involved deadly weapons and an enemy who was eager to kill me and my teammates. It would take only one bad encounter to change my life forever or end it for good. I certainly understood that. By pure repetition, the odds were stacking higher against us, every day.

Thankfully, on the SEAL teams, we have one another, this dynamic group of strong-willed individuals propelled into action by their own pride and commitment and by the powerful momentum of watching out for one another. Natural human instincts never disappear entirely, I suppose. Fear. Avoidance. Appropriate recognition of the risks involved. But none of those are a match for the power of the team.

We're not the only people who face death, of course. People are killed in car crashes and natural disasters. Children die of dreaded diseases every day. Death is a tragedy for everyone. But facing it as we do—violently, repeatedly, aware of its presence and its risks—has given me a far deeper appreciation of life's fragility and the need to live boldly and purposefully. And it's taught me the vital importance of having supportive people around. I don't fear death. My heart goes out to those who die alone.

WE FIGHT TO BE PART OF A BROTHERHOOD

I am committed to this team, the fellow warriors who fight at my side. They—the brotherhood we share—are why I serve.

Every great military unit is its own special tribe. For SEALs, the tribe is made up of the SEAL teams that share a common ethos or code: members subjugate individual needs to the needs of the group. And it's the good of the tribe that rises above the preferences of any individual. This is key. In the SEALs, we call it the brotherhood.

We teach this special unity in basic training and drive it home every single day after that: "Take care of your buddy." "Team before individual." "No one is ever left behind." These are nonnegotiables. We are not going to leave a fallen comrade on the battlefield, no matter what. Can the zealots we fight say that?

Some of the bravest acts I have ever witnessed—some of the most heroic acts I have ever performed—have occurred in the heat of battle in combat zones as a warrior put his own life in mortal danger to help a besieged team member to safety. I've seen guys run into live fire. I've seen them dance across IEDs. I've seen these heroes barrel headlong in the direction of falling mortar shells. I've even done some of those things myself. And the reason was always the same: a love of country expressed through a commitment to teammates. The two are so intertwined as to be inseparable.

More than once I've seen a soldier in trouble, concerned less for himself and more for his team, selflessly shouting across a battlefield or into a radio, demanding that his teammates not risk their lives to pull him out just yet. "Do NOT advance. I repeat. Do NOT advance."

The ultimate expression of this was our teammate Mikey, who ended up jumping on a grenade to save his buddies' lives. It's one thing to get shot. You don't know if the bullet is going to hit you when you hear gunfire and see an enemy taking aim. We've all heard cracks. I swear I've even felt bullets going past me. But I never thought, "Okay, let me jump onto one of those."

Mikey actually did.

He saw the grenade on the roof. He could tell it was about to go off. He recognized the damage that it could do to his teammates who were standing nearby. He selflessly threw his body on it, saving his teammates and friends. All we can do is guess what Mikey was thinking. He was never able to say. But I'm betting he understood exactly what he was dying for when he jumped on that grenade.

And I'm sure Mikey had never discussed that possibility or predicted how he might respond. It was inherent inside of him somewhere. It came from his heart, was displayed in his actions, and lived on far longer than words.

When death occurs on the battlefield, we send the fallen

off properly. Military funerals are different from any other funerals I have ever been to. When I was growing up, I attended funerals for my uncle and various older relatives. I remember the tear-filled eulogies and the family gathering together for old-style Irish wakes. There was always a retrospective of the person's life, recalling their accomplishments, the role they played in the family, and how they enjoyed spending their leisure time. Those funerals were sad, but also meaningful gatherings.

Military funerals are on another level entirely. The way we say good-bye to our fallen—the flag-draped coffin, the deceased in a dress uniform, people acknowledging the ultimate sacrifice—comes together in a reverent way that is almost indescribable. You can't attend a military funeral and not feel it. The entire experience is packed with significance. The respect is palpable.

There is the recognition that this person and his sacrifice are part of something much larger. There is the understanding that he made the sacrifices necessary to serve his country. If he died fighting for the country, there is profound reverence for that ultimate sacrifice. There is the confidence that his fight will be carried on by his dedicated teammates. And in far too many instances, there is the tragedy that he died so young.

The first time I experienced a full-uniform, pomp-and-circumstance military funeral, a range of emotions rushed through me. That roar of powerful feelings didn't frighten me.

It didn't give me pause or reason to question my own choices. Instead, as I listened to "Taps" and stood among the throngs of other uniformed warriors, I felt emboldened, which I suppose is the point. I couldn't help but think as the service continued, "Wow, if I have to go out early, *that* is the way to go."

OUR TOUR IS COMPLETE, WHATEVER COMES NEXT

I've had many people talk to me recently and say, "It must be painful to see things unraveling with all the work you guys have done." I have to say, I don't feel that way at all.

Maybe that's because none of what's happened since our troops began withdrawing has surprised me. All of us in the arena knew this was going to happen. It was just a matter of when. If we stayed over there forever, we might be able to manage it indefinitely. But we're not staying forever. If we leave, it's going to degrade. In earlier wars, we left troops behind—seemingly forever—on bases in Germany, South Korea, and Japan. But I don't know anyone who expects that to be repeated in Iraq and Afghanistan.

I don't worry about it though, not for a single second. In the window of time that we were over there, our warriors completed the job spectacularly. I can say that with a great deal of confidence. The people I was fighting against were bad by my standards. The people I was fighting beside were great.

We advanced the ball. We moved the needle. Use whatever analogy you like. We achieved what was asked of us. What the long-term fallout will be from the time we spent there—now, that's a question I'm interested in.

In many ways, the simplicity of being a warrior is a gift. I don't mean that in a mindless way, but even the most thoughtful warriors don't choose the fight for themselves. We take our orders. We accept our duty. We might choose where the actual fighting is going to start geographically. We might choose our own firing positions. *Why* we fight is a personal decision. *Where* we fight and *when* we fight—those calls are inevitably made far above our pay grade.

TRIDENT TAKEAWAYS

- We fight to protect our nation.
- We fight to support our brothers.
- We accept the risks willingly because we fight for a larger cause.

CHAPTER 7

EVERYONE MUST SERVE

When I read Winston Churchill in college, I knew immediately that service was my calling.

My senior year in college, my father mailed me a copy of Churchill's memoir *My Early Life*. I didn't know very much about Churchill. I knew he'd been the prime minister of England during World War II. I knew the British people were inspired by his fearlessness during the war and ultimately turned on him, voting him out of office after the danger had passed. He was England's prime sheepdog. But until my father sent that book, I'd never read anything Churchill had written, and I had no idea what his young life was like.

In the book, Churchill recounted his days at the Royal Military Academy at Sandhurst, the West Point of the British Army, and his many exploits as a young, frontline officer participating in combat missions in Cuba, South Africa, and the Sudan.

"Here," he wrote of an early trip to the battlefield, "was a place where real things were going on. Here was a scene of vital action. Here was a place where anything might happen. Here was a place where something would certainly happen."

In heart-pounding detail, he laid out his own personal inspirations and explained the strategies behind his battlefield moves. He loved to psyche out the enemy and to use whatever limited resources he had to his best advantage.

Young Churchill had a sense of purpose that was unequivocal. He set high standards for himself. He felt an unbridled thrill going into battle and adjusted as well as he could to returning home. He clearly loved his men. He had hopes and disappointments about Britain's large but fading empire. He had a great way with words. "My education," he wrote, "was interrupted only by my schooling." I could definitely relate to that. To the twenty-one-year-old me, romantic adventure jumped off every page.

Everything he did seemed important and exciting, even getting up in the morning.

"There is nothing like the dawn," he wrote. "The quarter of an hour before the curtain is lifted upon an unknowable situation is an intense experience of war. Was the ridge held by the enemy or not? Were we riding through the gloom into thousands of ferocious savages? Every step might be deadly.

Yet there was no time for much precaution. The regiment was coming on behind us, and dawn was breaking. It was already half-light as we climbed the slope. What should we find at the summit? For cool, tense excitement I commend such moments."

I swear he could have been speaking directly to me.

"Come on now all you young men, all over the world," he implored. "You are needed more than ever now to fill the gap of a generation shorn by the war. You have not an hour to lose. You must take your place in Life's fighting line."

I knew right then I had to serve. I gave up all thought of Wall Street and began applying to the SEALs. But was that just a personal career choice? Or is service a responsibility everyone must share? How does service to country stack up against service to family, community, political party, or faith? What about serving the "cause" of wealth creation, artistic expression, or personal enjoyment? Aren't those among the values and freedoms our troops are fighting for? It's time we as a nation sorted all this out. We need a new vocabulary of service.

HELP YOURSELF BY HELPING OTHERS

I know two of life's most important secrets. Being in the military, I've had a chance to experience the power of both of them. One is the secret to a rich life, and the other is the secret to a pain-free life.

I won't drag this out and keep you guessing.

The secret to a rich life has nothing to do with money. Money gives you options, which is important, but it rarely leads directly to happiness or richness of life. The secret to a rich life is good company. It's the people you surround yourself with, the peers you hold, the colleagues you choose, the folks you associate with, the strangers you turn into friends. That's what gives you a rich life.

People influence one another. That's obvious, isn't it? To some extent, we all conform our behavior to the behavior of those around us—our families, neighbors, colleagues, and friends. Without realizing it, each of us becomes our own personal math equation—the sum of all the people we surround ourselves with. We aren't always cognizant of it, but it is an unavoidable fact. So the company we keep is vitally important.

One thing that was so great about being in the SEALs was the world-class company I got to keep. We could be on a rooftop in Iraq. It could be 126 degrees outside. We're wading in pools of black tar because the sun has melted it. Mortar rounds are coming in, and still I remember raucous laughter from all four corners of the roof. Gripes and complaints too. We were in as hideous a location as you could ever find on earth. But the heavy air was filled with a whole lot more laughter than complaints. That's how enriching the company was.

Guys like Cam, who would regale us with riotous stories from his days as a professional juggler. Guys like Ro, who kept his focus on his gun and virtually never cracked a smile. Guys like Smitty, who held court like a late-night TV host, no matter how dire the situation was. Try as he did, Smitty could never shake Ro's concentration.

Laughing while ducking fire may seem odd, but no less a figure than Winston Churchill understood the phenomenon. "Laugh a little and teach your men to laugh," he advised. "Get good humor under fire. War is a game that's played with a smile. If you can't smile, grin. If you can't grin, keep out of the way till you can." None of that's possible if you're surrounded by the wrong people. Luckily, I've found my fellow SEALs to be excellent company.

The sooner you recognize the importance of company, the richer your life will be. I'm positive of this. Take an eighteen-year-old version of me. Not married. No kids. Nothing but time on my hands and an invitation to the Playboy Mansion on a Friday night. Plop me in a limousine to the Hollywood Hills. The catch is it's packed with a bunch of knuckleheads I don't want to spend time with. Even with a huge house full of the most beautiful women waiting at the end of the ride, I'm not interested. I'd rather stay home. Whatever fun I would have at the ultimate guys' paradise would be ruined by the idiots I had to hang out with all night.

There's no place good enough to justify bad company. And there is no set of circumstances bad enough that good company can't save it.

Playboy Mansion. Rooftop in Iraq. I rest my case.

Here's the second secret: the secret to a pain-free life is to think of others before yourself. If you think of others' needs and focus on other people's suffering, if your first question to yourself is "How can I help?"—you won't experience any real pain in your life.

I don't just mean you can avoid some kind of mental pain. If you are thinking of others before yourself, you'll discover you're far too busy to fixate on yourself.

There's a lot of need out there. There are many people you know who could use your attention. If you're someone who approaches the world unselfishly, believe me, you'll have no trouble finding people to love, support, and serve. If you're thinking of others first, it's almost impossible to obsess on your own dissatisfactions and complaints. You can't think about your own problems when you're thinking of someone else.

I know religious vocations are way down in this country. But my aunt is a Catholic nun in New York City—Sister

Teresa. She's the happiest person I've ever met in my life. Truthfully, I don't think she's thought of herself one day ever. She thinks of others from the time she gets up in the morning until the time she goes to bed at night. She thinks of children who need help, older people who need a little attention, programs that she can create to help people of all ages experience better lives. That is just what she does. She wants them to find God, for sure, and that is often the outgrowth of the work she does. Mainly, she sincerely wants people to thrive however they can, and she is always there to help. I can tell you she is one hundred percent pain-free. Nothing bothers her. If she experiences something you or I might consider pain, I don't believe it would bother her. She lives a clean, ideal life because she never thinks of herself first.

I think of my college classmates. When we graduated, people pursued different careers. But the single most popular choice was moving to New York to work in finance. I guess they never read Churchill. I don't think any of them made a poor decision, nor am I suggesting that anyone was being self-centered, money-focused, or insufficiently concerned about saving the world. I don't make those judgments. The finance industry—banking, brokerage houses, accounting firms, the many, many aspects of Wall Street—that's the engine of our economy. I get that. But my buddies learned to make something, and I went to find out what I was made of.

Their careers provided many opportunities. They had the chance to build businesses, create jobs, support their local communities, and be impact leaders in their own right by devoting their talents to our economy. I devoted mine to something different, the defense and protection of the United States.

At the time, I certainly didn't realize how potent a choice that was—to perform a job where your role is to serve in every possible way. You're asking your family to sacrifice for your service. You will sacrifice yourself for your teammates—maybe in the ultimate way, but at a minimum to make sure they're taken care of. Even stateside, at home between deployments, there's not a teammate of mine who couldn't call me any time of day or night and ask for help. Whatever the circumstances, I would be there.

I hope everybody has friends like that. I have dozens of friends I can call tomorrow and make almost any request.

"Jihadis are after me. I need help."

"My kid needs an operation. Can you help us raise some money?"

"Our roof just blew off in a tornado. Can you gather up some guys and lend a hand?"

Now, I may not be the guy nailing the shingles back on a roof—I'd probably screw that up. But I'd be all in, and I know my guys would be too. They wouldn't even need to be briefed on the details. They'd say, "Where are you? There's a flight that goes out tonight. I'll be on it." I think this makes me one of the richest guys in the world.

EVERYONE SHOULD BE REQUIRED TO SERVE SOMEHOW

The power of good company. The importance of considering others first. They are both outer-directed. They require thinking of others before you think of yourself. People in the military know about that. They live it every day. So do many teachers, firefighters, police officers, clergy, and others who have dedicated their lives in an outward direction. But why stop there?

I'm not suggesting we need to be a nation of full-time, professional caregivers and service providers. I'm not coming out against business, capitalism, personal artistic expression, or anything of the kind. Those are all good things. Abandoning them wouldn't be practical, and it wouldn't be smart. It certainly wouldn't leave us with a very robust economy, help us compete with countries around the world, or enable us to do many of the good things we want to do.

But everyone—and I mean *everyone*—should have the experience of service, the chance to help others in a concerted fashion and learn the awesome power of doing just that. The best route there, I am convinced, is a mandatory term of public service for all young Americans.

Despite our challenges and shortcomings, we are hugely blessed in America. Just look around if you haven't lately at what's between those two great oceans: a beautiful and wildly diverse landscape. An economy that supports 325 million people at a standard of living unimaginable by historic standards. Exploding technologies that make many things easier and more enjoyable. Opportunities for education, recreation, entrepreneurship, and careers. Yes, we have our nagging problems, our disappointing leaders, and our pockets of real genuine poverty. But there's a reason so many people are still desperate to move here, and it isn't just our movies, video games, job opportunities, and unique way of life. It's the freedom and hopefulness that America still stands for everywhere in the world.

I have traveled to many different places I wouldn't want to live. I have gotten to know many structures, rules, and belief systems that I wouldn't want to be a part of. And I certainly know this to be true: the core idea of freedom is so rare and potent, very few people who live here in America truly appreciate its deep resonance. You can say what you want to in America. For the most part, you can do what you want. You can be who you want. You can believe what you want. Where else in the world does this ring so true?

The thing that scares our enemies far more than any weapons system we possess is our arsenal of freedom and our deeply entrenched commitment to it. This really is who we are as a country and what we've fought so voraciously for in history. These freedoms—freedom of thought, freedom of speech, freedom of expression, freedom to do pretty much as we damn well please—these are what inflame our enemies. Our liberty starts with the Bill of Rights and bubbles up from there. It's the single most gripping inspiration for opportunity and liberty in the world. Others would do anything to enjoy the same freedoms, and our enemies would do anything they can to obliterate it. Our freedom bothers them far more than our affluence, more than our faith, more than everything else about what it means to be American. I am convinced of this. They may claim we live lives of excess, that we are god-less, weak, and any number of other claims that they cannot abide. But they are far more frightened of our freedom than anything else.

Our enemies want to destroy modern civilization. If they can do that and fifty of them are left standing, they'd be happy about it. Our enemies want to end what we enjoy. The fact that the very architecture of our society is based on some of those fundamental principles means it's worth saving.

That's how powerful this freedom is.

Yet most of the time, we hardly appreciate it. We run

through our lives oblivious. Busy. Striving. Focused. Pressured by the day-to-day. Many Americans have become enormously me-focused—looking out for themselves and their families and that's about it. What's good for me? How can I get something more than I'm already getting? What can society help me achieve? Perhaps it's because of the comforts we live with or because we fight for these freedoms, the Revolutionary War, was nearly two and a half centuries ago. Whatever the reason, more and more, we lean on big government, big companies, and big technology—expecting these large social forces to support and defend us, and take care of a whole array of little challenges in our lives. It's a dangerous place to be, holding so many expectations that others are supposed to fulfill.

We need something to revive, to reinvigorate, the great American spirit that landed us here in the first place—that powerful fuel that kept us moving ever upward all these years. We need something to reverse the complacency and softness that inevitably sets in after too much comfort. We need the rededication and bonding that only service can provide.

Mandatory public service for all young Americans.

Everyone.

One year.

Full-time.

When someone says "serve," most people think "military."

That's the first word that pops to mind. That's not what I'm talking about. I want to rescue the idea of public service from all the harsh feelings about a military draft. And I think it's doable. If we create a thoughtful system of universal public service, we eliminate the knee-jerk objections: "I don't believe in war. I don't like people yelling at me. I'm not physically or mentally or psychologically or spiritually prepared for military life." Then we can get to the benefits of universal service without all the baggage of a draft. Without the resentment. Without the unfairness. Without the conscientious objections or the high moral outrage that any military draft is sure to generate. Some people will always be antimilitary. No one can be against the idea of service if the system is fair, flexible, and universal. Let's take all the grounds for objection away.

Working in a soup kitchen, repairing homes for hurricane victims, helping poor kids learn to read, cleaning up after an oil spill, fortifying an eroding beach or a shrinking forest, teaching computer skills to laid-off adults, helping new immigrants get settled, providing assistance to wounded veterans, or enlisting in a military unit. The possibilities are nearly endless. I could give you about a thousand others. But it should be something real that involves genuine service to others and helps to make America a better place. Imagine how that universal service would change the national mindset and all the good works that could get done if everyone spent a full year just helping others. You can't say we don't have enough need in this country.

I understand there are needs abroad. Meeting them is a wonderful thing to do. But when it comes to this year of youthful service, let's keep it on our shores. After that, if you are so inclined, join the Peace Corps, become a missionary, run an antimalaria campaign in Malawi, or build a water project in Indonesia. We still have major needs in America, and this year of universal service should bond young Americans to that.

The simple truth of the matter is there isn't any one way or even any one time to serve. Let's just say you graduate high school. Instead of launching right into college, go serve for a year. You want to go to college first? Great. Defer your service four years. You want to break up college with a service year? Terrific. The way I imagine it, there would have to be some outside deadline to get this idea to work, perhaps you must serve your country for one year before your twenty-fifth birthday. You want to extend your service beyond a year? You bet. Do another year. I think a lot of people would.

There'd be no out, no pass, no other path to take. Death, taxes, service. All unavoidable. And service should be the least objectionable of the three. It has far more choice built in than the other two. It could be military service, a Reserve or National Guard unit. It could be working with a government agency. It could be signing on with the Red Cross, Habitat for Humanity, Teach for America, or one of thousands of other groups whose primary purpose is helping Americans in need.

Some of the details we'll still have to work out. We'll have to figure out how much to pay people. A subsistence wage, I would suggest—enough to live frugally and not much more, which is how we compensate entry-level enlisted people in the military. There will be logistical challenges as well, though not as many as you'd expect. We'll have to figure out what to do with people who are disabled, or have young children to care for, or have genuine, pressing obligations—there are always ways to serve while meeting the real responsibilities they have to meet. But there should be no permanent exemptions for the well-to-do, the college educated, the politically connected, the children of celebrities, or anyone else who has the genuine capacity for service. We mustn't take the *universal* out of universal service.

Would universal service cost money? Sure, it would. A lot. But we can afford it. We spend money on so many things that produce far less good than what a system of universal service would provide—benefits to the nation; people being served; and, I daresay, most of all, to the people doing the serving. There could hardly be a better bargain in Washington than this one. The results would be plain for everyone to see.

AMERICANS WANT TO SERVE

The spirit of service is already deeply embedded in us as Americans. In recent years I have been proud to watch young Americans—and not-so-young people—swoop in whenever disaster struck somewhere, almost no matter what kind of disaster or where it occurred. Tornadoes in Oklahoma. Mudslides in California. Hurricanes along the Gulf of Mexico. If anything, the spirit of volunteerism is on the rise.

After 9/11, firefighters, police officers, and other first responders descended by the thousands on New York City, volunteering to help with the rescue and recovery at Ground Zero, and it wasn't just uniformed personnel. Schoolchildren donated their lunch money. Construction companies sent building supplies. Random Americans delivered memorial posters and sympathy cards and offered prayers. All of these acts of service contained the same message: "We are here for you. We care."

If anything, the impulse was even stronger after Hurricane Katrina. When the federal levees broke and 80 percent of New Orleans was underwater, people rushed in from across the country—college students, church groups, older couples, young families sacrificing their vacation time. The FEMA money helped. But it was all those thoughtful, individual actions that truly pulled that waterlogged city out of the muck. At the same time, decent people around the country opened their hearts and homes to Katrina refugees. And the giving continued long after the headlines moved on. Charmed by the city and its vibrant people, some volunteers even moved there permanently, securing the revival of one of America's cultural jewels. Tell me what other country would give like that.

And check out what's been happening in Detroit. After decades of industrial decline, some experts were giving up America's Motor City for dead. But now entrepreneurs, artists, and even farmers have come together to breathe new life into Detroit. These people know how to build things, and I tell you, they are building again. Filling old auto plants with new high-tech businesses. Turning blighted blocks into organic urban farms. Even the auto industry is shifting into a higher gear. I have friends in Detroit who have started a very successful luxury-lifestyle consumer-products company in a former mothballed factory. Under a classic American brand name, Shinola, they are making high-design watches, urban bicycles, and leather goods—and receiving buzz around the world. Even top Swiss watchmakers have been impressed by the quality of their workmanship.

There are so many ways to serve beyond what government and private agencies do already. The needs are almost endless. The results can be immediate, practical, visible, and highly satisfying. The chance to look at a rebuilt house or listen to a student read aloud for the first time—what could be more enriching than that? Don't tell me these aren't life-changing experiences for the server and the served.

THE SELFISH BENEFITS OF SERVICE

As is almost always the case when it comes to serving others, the givers will benefit as much if not more than the recipients will. Think of the training opportunities. Think of confidence and the worldliness such an experience would build. Think of the new parts of the American landscape our young people could experience.

Getting out of the nest and away from home is a benefit all its own. That's one of the great things public service can offer. Ideally, your service shouldn't be in your own home-town, although there's nothing wrong with being generous at home. If possible, go somewhere. The program should be designed that way. If you grew up in New York City, your service might be in Ohio, California, or some other place that gets you to a different region with a different socioeconomic status and class than you come from. Guaranteed, it'll open your eyes.

The group dynamic is hugely important here. The service year would be spent working with a group of young people, probably from all corners of the country. This in itself is an opportunity that can't be overstressed. We have learned a lot about this in the military: unit cohesion, we call it—or in the SEALs, the brotherhood. It's the bond that grows among a group of people who take on a difficult duty together and come to rely on one another in deep and unexpected ways.

Not everyone would have to shave his head, wear a plain white T-shirt, and be yelled at by a barking drill instructor, though I do believe some of that is a strength of the military. In the military, no matter where you come from, your head's going to look exactly like the guy and the gal next to you at boot camp. You're wearing the same T-shirt, the same ugly pants, the same uncomfortable pair of shoes walking through the same exact chow line every day.

There's a reason we do those things in the military. We break people down to a piece of raw clay. Those challenges together say, "We're all the same." Then we build everyone up to the place where we can perform at the highest level together. It takes the individual out of the equation and brings the culture to the forefront.

It's hard not to bond in circumstances like that.

Some critics are sure to complain. They will moan about the service options. So let's create new ones. They will complain about careers delayed. Those careers will still be there a year from now. They will complain we are taking jobs away from Americans who need them. So let's not do that. These service positions should be important work that isn't already being done. It's value added. It's society improved. It's a way to meet needs that are currently being neglected. The added bonus is that young people will experience personal growth and a connection to our nation that cannot be learned in high school or in college or in most entry-level jobs.

This is too good an idea to be sidetracked by its critics. Let's get on with it—now.

Imagine unleashing the power of American service on some of the most challenging problems our nation faces now. I get excited just thinking about all the possibilities.

As Abraham Lincoln put it: "To ease another's heartache is to forget one's own." Almost like magic, it works every time.

A rich, pain-free life, guaranteed.

TRIDENT TAKEAWAYS

- We are hugely blessed in America and owe something in return.
- There is no one way to serve, but everyone must.
- Serving benefits the server as much as the served.

CHAPTER 8

BRIDGING THE MILITARY-CIVILIAN DIVIDE

The story of "The Sheep, the Wolves, and the Sheepdogs" has become a staple of SEAL field exercises and special-operator gatherings across the country. I first heard it from Lieutenant Colonel Dave Grossman, a warrior peer of mine who is one of our great scholar-soldiers. Dave didn't make up this story and told me he first heard it from a retired colonel who'd fought in Vietnam, and the colonel most likely heard it from someone else. Wherever it originated, it's a part of SEAL culture now, and it tells an important truth.

Most of the people in our society are sheep. They are kind, gentle, productive creatures who only hurt one another by accident. The vast majority of Americans certainly fall into this category. They don't cause much fuss. They try to do what's right and aren't big risk takers. They aren't looking to change the world in any dramatic way.

In this context, there is nothing insulting about calling someone a sheep. It's the day-to-day reality for the millions of people who go to work, support their families, enjoy their friends, and go about their normal business.

Then there are the wolves. The wolves prey on the sheep without mercy. All across history, there have been evil people in the world. They are the criminals, despots, dictators, domestic abusers, con artists—anyone who uses power, trickery, or force to injure or exploit the weakness of regular people. The wolves will attack the weakest sheep for any reason at all.

Thankfully, there are far more sheep than wolves in the world. The level of the wolves' viciousness rises and falls over time. But sadly, the wolves do keep coming around.

Finally, there are the sheepdogs.

My brother SEALs and I, we are sheepdogs. We protect the flock from the wolves.

It isn't just people in the military. Police officers, firefighters, and paramedics are sheepdogs too. Some sheepdogs don't have official titles. They just go through life protecting the victims from the perpetrators, even at risk to themselves. Sheepdogs are ready to fight whenever they have to. Not just ready, they are eager to fight. They live to fight. In fact, they like nothing better than to fight. Navy SEALs are the alpha sheepdogs, seeking out wolves anywhere around the world. Were it not for the sheepdogs, the sheep would be slaughtered by the wolves.

At times of threat and trouble, the sheep love the sheep-dogs. They call them heroes. They honor their service. They recognize what terrible straits they'd be in were it not for the courageous sheepdogs who put their own comfort and safety on the line to protect the mild and peaceful from the aggressive and malicious.

Inevitably, the sheepdogs are never appreciated for long. The trouble passes. Memories fade. The sheep forget the danger. Soon enough, the sheepdogs start seeming a little threatening on their own. In fact, they almost look like wolves, don't they? Same thick coat. Same forward eyes. Same long fangs. Eventually, the sheep turn on the sheepdogs. The sheepdogs are heroes when the wolves are nearby. But when the wolves are gone, the sheep start to wonder why they need sheepdogs at all.

SOME SERVE, MOST DON'T

Are you in the military? Do you know anyone who is? For more Americans than ever, the answer is a flat-out no. The statistics are startling. Less than one half of 1 percent of Americans are now serving in the armed forces. In World War II, the number was 12 percent.

Let me put it another way: if I were to line up two hundred random Americans, maybe one of them would be

active-duty Army, Navy, Air Force, Coast Guard, or Marines.
Or maybe not. There's an even chance. Go ahead and do the
math. One-point-four million men and women are serving
now, according to the Defense Manpower Data Center. The
U.S. population is more than 320 million. My calculator says
.4375 percent in uniform.

Even if we count the nation's twenty-two million
veterans—every living American who has *ever* been in the
military—the number is still small, 7.3 percent. And it's falling fast. The youngest Vietnam veterans are now in their six-
ties. Most veterans of the Korean War, the ones who are still
living, are well into their eighties, and sadly, the last World
War II vets won't be with us much longer. Thirty years from
now, the U.S. Department of Veterans Affairs estimates, there
will be only fourteen million living veterans. Many Americans may not ever know a single one. It'll be more difficult to
round up a quorum at the American Legion or the Veterans
of Foreign Wars posts, or to find enough people to march in
the Veterans Day parades.

It may not seem that our veteran population is decreas-
ing if you walk down the street in San Diego, California, or
Norfolk, Virginia, or Killeen, Texas, or Fayetteville, North
Carolina, or any of our country's great military communities. But these are distinct and special places, different in
many respects from other American cities and towns. There's

a reason they're called "military" towns. The frank displays of patriotism. The shared concerns of waiting spouses. The support that's second nature in any military community. The welcome-home and come-back-safely house parties. The low-level anxiety, rising with each new wave of deployments. Despite their varied geography, military towns have a whole lot more in common with one another than with other ordinary American communities.

If you drill down into the demographics, they tell a fascinating tale. It's not just that members of the military end up in a small number of geographical locales—it's more about where they come from. Some regions, groups, and economic classes join the military in numbers out of proportion to their actual size. The rural south, industrial midwest, and working-class neighborhoods in some big cities have been sending far more than their share into battle. But good luck finding anyone to salute in Beverly Hills, Chicago's Miracle Mile, or Manhattan's Upper East Side. Year in and year out, folks in some zip codes are perfectly content letting others do the fighting for them.

There are exceptions, of course. Some Ivy Leaguers and folks from upper-crust families proudly join up and serve with great distinction. Lieutenant John F. Kennedy, a Harvard graduate from one of America's wealthiest families, had what may be the most famous small-craft engagement in U.S.

naval history when his PT boat encountered a Japanese destroyer on August 1, 1943. The future president downplayed his widely reported heroism: "It was involuntary," he said. "They sank my boat."

SOLDIERS JOIN THE FAMILY BUSINESS

What I find most impressive—in a good and bad way—is how the military has become such a family business. When we speak of brothers-in-arms today, frequently we are talking about actual kin. My dad wasn't in the military, but several of my uncles served our country. And my paternal grandfather, First Lieutenant Thomas Henry Rorke, was a navigator on a B-24 Liberator who was killed in the Pacific theater in World War II, as many Army Air Corps officers were. Stories about Grandpa Rorke definitely planted ideas about enlisting in my preadolescent head.

Saving Private Ryan was set during the invasion of Normandy in World War II, but that true story could have happened today. Four Ryan brothers served, but families like the Ryans are more common than they've ever been. If one family member is serving, chances are high that others are too. My SEAL buddy Dave has two other brothers and a brother-in-law on the SEAL teams. He grew up in the

Staten Island borough of New York City in a family filled with boys so raucous they roped off part of the backyard for a boxing ring. Besides the three SEALs, the family also included a couple of firefighters. We all know families like Dave's.

Brother-brother SEAL combinations—even brother-brother-brother SEALs—have become common now. We have cousin-cousin combos, father-son combos, uncle-nephew combos. We are still waiting for our first grandfather-father-son legacy on the SEAL teams, but it'll happen, I'm sure of it. Relatives literally follow one another to the recruitment office or into ROTC.

Credit the Pew Research Center for putting a number on this trend: 79 percent of American veterans have an immediate family member who is serving or has served in the military. In what other field would that be true? None that I can think of.

This widening civilian-military divide is not random. There are practical and historical reasons for the separation. Some are economic. For many young people from less wealthy families, the military provides a great ladder of upward mobility. Some young people choose to serve for cultural reasons. Pride in military service is more deeply ingrained in some communities and it self-perpetuates. But the biggest reason of all for the civilian-military divide is the historical resentment toward the military draft.

In fact, America has a long but uneasy relationship with the concept of required military service. There has always been willingness among many Americans, sometimes even an eagerness, to join the military in times of peril or war. But when "forced" or "mandatory" or "compulsory" is added to the equation—when "voluntary enlistment" gives way to "draft"—freedom-loving Americans have often been far more skittish. During the Revolutionary War, the thirteen colonies conscripted some men for militia duty or to fill state Continental Army units when the volunteer ranks grew thin. But the central government didn't have the authority to force anyone to serve, and most of the colonists couldn't imagine it any other way. President James Madison tried to create a national draft of forty thousand men during the War of 1812. Fierce opposition led by antiwar congressman Daniel Webster of New Hampshire blocked the "un-American" proposal before the first conscript was found.

It wasn't until the Civil War that America had anything resembling a real draft—both in the north and the south. Even then, the systems were rife with exemptions and loopholes. For one thing, conscripts on both sides could hire substitutes to serve for them. The vast majority of Civil War combatants were volunteers.

The first broad draft came in World War I. The war was so unpopular, only seventy-three thousand people volunteered for the Army's initial target of one million troops. President Woodrow Wilson decided he had no other choice. His new Selective Service Act of 1917 forbade substitutes and established a "liability for military service of all male citizens" between twenty-one and thirty-one years of age, later extended to eighteen and forty-five. Twenty-four million men registered. Nearly three million were called, including half a million recent immigrants. The force included blacks as well as whites, though they served in segregated units. The draft ended quickly, in 1918.

In 1940, after Germany invaded France, President Roosevelt signed the Selective Training and Service Act. After Pearl Harbor, as World War II expanded rapidly, the manpower demands were enormous. Two hundred thousand American men a month were inducted for a term that lasted as long as the war did. Ultimately, more than ten million men served, the vast majority of them draftees.

The war ended. The troops went home. The military needed far fewer bodies. But the draft never fully went away. Between the end of World War II and 1973, during times of peace and war, men were drafted to fill vacancies in the U.S. armed forces. One-point-one million men were drafted for the Korean War. During the Vietnam era, 2.2 million men were drafted for military service, and the draft was credited with "encouraging" many of the war's 8.7 million "volunteers."

As the Vietnam War raged on, the draft became a key flashpoint of opposition. It sparked huge protests on college campuses and in major cities across the United States. Millions avoided service, legally and not. Many, like future president Bill Clinton and future vice president Dick Cheney, won educational deferments. Others finagled stateside assignments with National Guard units. Some, like Mohammed Ali, objected to the war on moral or political grounds and faced serious legal consequences. Nearly a hundred thousand young men dodged the draft, mostly going to Canada. Richard Nixon ran for president in 1968 promising to end the draft, though it wasn't until near the end of the war in 1973 that the Selective Service announced there'd no longer be a draft. In that divided era, ending the draft was one of very few decisions in Washington that was greeted with almost universal relief.

But still. The end to compulsory military service had an unintended consequence, something we suffer from even today. It made the military less like a national commitment and more like just another job that some people wanted and many did not. With a draft, Americans were all being asked collectively to take action to protect our nation and all it stands for. Now, without compulsory service, a large percentage of the country inevitably decides not to serve. And those who do join are often doing so for the training, education benefits, or because civilian opportunities are hard to find in a tough economy.

That, in a nutshell, is how we became us and them.

TWO SEPARATE NATIONS BETWEEN THE SAME TWO OCEANS

Because of this place we're in, it can feel like military America is a separate country within a country, with civilian America existing someplace else. Some days it's as if the people who inhabit these two Americas hardly know each other anymore. How could they? They live, work, and hang out in totally different worlds.

Since the end of the draft, America has had an all-volunteer military. No one is forced to serve. Occasionally, some politician will float the idea of reinstating the draft, though the suggestion is usually made to push a larger point about an unpopular war or social inequality. Hardly anyone, in military or civilian life, really wants the draft to resume.

I know I don't. I wouldn't want to go into battle with teammates who don't want to be there. I want to fight beside guys who are all in. The draft caused so much resentment during Vietnam, I don't ever want to see that repeated again. Some people, let's be honest, just aren't cut out for military service. Dragging them onto the battlefield is a losing proposition. I'd rather find something else for them to do.

And there's no denying the many successes of our modern all-volunteer force. The U.S. military is indisputably the mightiest fighting force on earth, truly the most powerful in human history. So then, why should we care if our nation is protected by a professional military caste? For many reasons. This us-them division has isolated military families from civilian ones. Few families have a foot in both worlds, and as a nation, we are all left thinking more narrowly and factionally. How will our military families ever gain any fresh perspectives if everyone on the block or in the apartment complex is dealing with exactly the same things? At the same time, how can we expect the larger civilian communities to understand people they've never met, worked around, or lived near? It's not going to happen—mark my words.

Too big a division between the protectors and protected almost always leads to mistrust. Isn't that why many urban police departments require their officers to live within the city limits? Isn't that why sports fans usually root for the home team? Proximity breeds familiarity, which breeds support.

Basic fairness also dictates that we all share in the responsibility for protecting our country. When America had a draft, some eligible people managed to avoid enlisting through student deferments, medical exemptions, or other means. But many people from all walks of life still served. Not as many as in World War II—but young people from all parts of the country and various walks of life did go to Vietnam. Now too much of the burden is falling on too few shoulders.

Our unique freedom isn't free. It isn't just bestowed on us. We have to pay for it. I understand that and I think most Americans do too. Our government can provide the sophisticated equipment, the uniforms, even the soldiers' pay. But the men and women willing to serve are still the most crucial part of the military. And they often pay the price by risking their lives to protect our nation's freedom.

That's not right, even if recruits accepted it voluntarily. Most people pay taxes. Everyone has the right to vote (please, don't get me started on our pathetically low voter turnout!). We are all expected to obey the law. But our obligations as citizens shouldn't end there. Should we not all contribute more personally? Should defending this great nation really be the responsibility of 0.4375 percent? When confronted with numbers as stark as these, I'll bet even most civilians wouldn't think so. We'd simply be a better nation if more people had a direct stake in defending the country.

The way I have always looked at it is that military service is like a tax—an appropriate tax in my mind—for enjoying all the many blessings our country has to offer. It would be nice if everything were free. But the nation can't survive unless someone foots the bill, and that includes this most essential one.

THE FOUNDING FATHERS HATED HIRED GUNS

A professional military class also is inconsistent with our history and tradition. The founders of this country fought against establishing a self-perpetuating military class, separate from the rest of society. George Washington believed the army should be *of* the people, not just hired by them. "When we assumed the Soldier, we did not lay aside the Citizen," he said back when America was being created. The nation needed citizen-fighters, Samuel Adams agreed. "A standing Army, however necessary it may be at some times, is always dangerous to the Liberties of the People," he wrote in a 1776 letter to James Warren, a general in the Massachusetts militia who declined to serve in the Continental Army when he was offered a lower rank. "Soldiers are apt to consider themselves as a Body distinct from the rest of the Citizens." And vice versa, no doubt.

What the Founding Fathers warned so presciently about seems to be happening in America now with all the attendant consequences—especially a lack of mutual understanding, but also a failure to fully grasp the human consequences of any military engagement. A willingness to send our troops in without an exit plan, over and over again. When a family has a child who is serving, that family has a strong incentive to pay attention to what is going on in the world, and to be thoughtful about whether a political problem really calls for a military solution.

A general population that doesn't know the military, and a military that has trouble grasping how most civilians feel. A missing political coalition to support our military needs. Too little human connection between the civilian leaders who deliver the orders and the troops who are expected to execute them. This disconnect is disturbing. And it's vastly different from the traditional American way, forged in the earliest days of the republic.

I'm not the only one who finds this trend disquieting. Questions are already being raised by some of America's more independent military thinkers. Retired Army lieutenant general Karl Eikenberry, who commanded U.S. troops in Afghanistan, took a close look at this development. He and Stanford University history professor David Kennedy published their blunt conclusion in the *New York Times*: "The greatest challenge to our military is not from a foreign enemy—it's the widening gap between the American people and their armed forces."

We can't ignore it forever. There comes a time when you have too few sheepdogs and too many sheep.

WASHINGTON, THE VET-FREE ZONE

The picture is no brighter with America's elected officials. Look who we've been sending to Washington over the past few decades. In 1971, military veterans made up the vast majority of Congress with 72 percent in the House of Representatives and 78 percent in the Senate. Many of the members were World War II veterans and quite a few were veterans of the Korean War, though a trickle of Vietnam vets were starting to arrive.

Regardless of what era they were in uniform, whether in wartime or peacetime, ambitious politicians understood: some career in the military was considered almost a prerequisite for public service. It certainly provided a political leg up. And it just made sense. People in the military had already begun a career in service to the nation. Governing was a logical next step. Then the numbers began to slip. In 1981, military veterans made up 64 percent of the House and the Senate, somewhat lower but still a solid majority. Ten years later, in 1991, the percentage of veterans dropped further to 48 percent. And the numbers just kept falling. In 2001, veterans made up 30 percent of the two houses of Congress.

And that wasn't the bottom. It's hard to say where the bottom is. The 114th Congress, which took office at the beginning of 2015, hit an all-time low. Just 18 percent of the members were veterans—eighty-one men and women in the House of Representatives and thirteen in the Senate. That's a massive decline in less than half a century.

The Senate lost its last World War II veteran when New Jersey's Frank Lautenberg died in 2013. As recently as 1985, World War II vets made up nearly one-third of Congress. Pretty soon there won't be any Korean veterans left. There is a small uptick of young vets serving in Washington, men and women who served in the Gulf War and the wars in Afghanistan and Iraq. It's not enough to offset those who are dying or leaving, but at least it's something. The first of this new class was Representative Patrick Murphy, a Pennsylvania Democrat who came to Congress in 2007 and promptly made Iraq one of his key issues.

Groups like Iraq and Afghanistan Veterans of America have been recruiting a new generation to run for public office, and they've been having some successes. But still it's hard to imagine a return to the 1970s when more than two-thirds of Congress knew what it meant to put on a uniform.

Something similar has been happening in the White House, though the numbers are much smaller, so it's hard to make the same statistical case. There, the long line of veterans goes back to the very start of the country. George Washington, of course, was a veteran of the Revolutionary War. He helped to create the country that he presided over. There is no more impressive veteran-politician story than his.

Two of our last three presidents, Obama and Clinton, were not veterans (George W. Bush served in the Texas Air National Guard). Clinton and Obama interrupted a long line of veteran-presidents. George H. W. Bush, Ronald Reagan, Jimmy Carter, Richard Nixon, John Kennedy, Dwight Eisenhower, and Harry Truman. You then have to go all the way back to Franklin Delano Roosevelt, who had serious health issues, to find the last U.S. president who didn't serve our country. This is no recent fluke. Of the nation's forty-four presidents before Obama, Clinton, and FDR, all but nine served in the military or their state's militias.

I want to put this as respectfully as I can. For my two cents, our greatest presidents have been veterans of the military.

OUR POLITICAL LEADERS NEED MORE SKIN IN THE GAME

Does it truly matter that fewer veterans are finding their way to Washington? Can't civilian leaders be just as ardent in responding to military needs? The commander in chief isn't a commander in the military sense. Neither is the secretary of defense. The constitution says the nation's armed forces should be run by civilians.

True enough.

But Congress and the president together determine all policies and funding for the U.S. armed forces. Every new weapons system, every new warship, and every new war-fighting technology has to pass through their powerful hands. The Senate confirms the defense secretary. The military budget has to be passed by both houses of Congress before it reaches the president's desk. Our Constitution says wars are declared by Congress, and then waged by a president with authority granted to him from Capitol Hill. And when service members are discharged or they retire, it is Congress that funds and sets the major policies at the U.S. Department of Veterans Affairs—the sprawling executive agency responsible for most veteran care. The GI Bill, VA loans, post-traumatic stress disorder (PTSD) treatments—you name it. If it has to do with the military policies or people, chances are Congress and the president are intimately involved.

I'd say this to anyone in uniform, past or present: you may not be interested in politics, but politics is definitely interested in you.

There's no denying that the military gets some terrific support from lifelong civilians in office. But military service matters. Where you've been has to affect how you feel and what you know. Congressmen and senators who've worn the uniform—even presidents—have an instinctive understanding that is deeper than those who never have.

To get a better sense of this, all you need to do is look at the increasing inadequacy of the Department of Veterans Affairs. I'm sure there are people inside that sprawling bureaucracy who work hard and care about our veterans. But why are so many military families still struggling so desperately? Why are so many on public assistance? Clearly, their needs are not getting met through the official veterans' programs. Much of the gap is now being filled by forty-eight thousand nonprofit veterans-aid groups. The number of groups is staggering. Large and small, national and local, these groups do amazing work. There are so many, it's hard to single out just a few. Some I support are Soldier Socks, Troops Direct, and the Navy SEAL Foundation. It is great that organizations like these are stepping up. It would be even greater if the need for them weren't so severe.

What if half of Congress came from the ranks of the military? How might this positively affect our troops? I can guess this much. Their intuitive understanding of veterans' health care, the frontline impact of sequestration, or the lurking dangers of PTSD would change the status quo. It's not just their grasp of specific issues that impacts our nation's veterans. It's also about the approach. One thing veteran-lawmakers have been good at is working across the political aisle. It's a skill the military teaches—working with people different from yourself. No one's better than a vet at asking, "What interests do we share that can help get this mission done?"

The bipartisan efforts to reform the veterans' health system were an encouraging example of this attitude. In 2014, Republicans and Democrats in the House and the Senate came together—*imagine that*—to present President Obama with a $16.3 billion reform package, which he promptly signed. "Our veterans don't have time for politics," the president said. Such cooperation was so rare that Senate Veterans Affairs Committee chairman Bernie Sanders joked with Obama as he picked up a pen, "Do you remember how to sign these things?"

"Just barely," the president said. "I don't get enough practice. We should do it more often."

If only.

There is still far to go. Civilian and military America need to be better acquainted, the sheep and the sheepdogs. We are more alike than different. We all want our nation to succeed. Imagine how much we could achieve if we kept working together as one.

TRIDENT TAKEAWAYS

➤ Whichever side of the divide you're on,
reach toward the other.

➤ The draft was hated but had its benefits.

➤ Hire a vet.

CHAPTER 9

THE DEBT WE OWE
OUR WARRIORS

You don't see too many special operators out in public in uniform—almost none, actually. We do have our own secret radar that helps us recognize one another, even in large crowds. We'll catch an eye, nod a wordless hello. Sometimes, we'll have a quiet reunion. Most of the time, though, we just move on. We don't like calling attention to ourselves.

As a SEAL, I have only two places I wear my uniform off base. One is to a wedding, which is a terrific reason to be in uniform, raising my sword with a buddy and his bride to celebrate a wonderful moment in their lives. The second reason is for a funeral. I've been to more funerals than I can remember in the last decade. I've lost track of the number, but it far exceeds the number of weddings I've attended. I wear my uniform as a sign of respect. It's a mark of reverence and emphasizes to me and others that this is a profound and somber event, especially when the departed has been taken in battle.

People definitely notice military uniforms today, wherever they are worn.

I can tell you this much from personal experience: there has not been a single time that I've been in uniform off base that my back hasn't nearly been bruised from people slapping it so hard.

"Thank you for your service," they say.

"We're pulling for you guys over there."

"Come back safely—and soon."

This isn't just for SEALs. All people in the military get those atta-boys these days. I notice a lot of Army personnel walking through airports in uniform, changing planes in Dallas, Denver, Chicago, Charlotte, or Pittsburgh. I see uniformed Navy guys and gals moving between boot camp and their first duty stations. They're constantly being stopped. It's rare that someone doesn't come over to shake a hand, pick up a meal tab, or just say hello.

It's great that people express their gratitude to those who serve our country. It's always nice to hear thanks. For any soldier, being allowed to board a plane first or being treated to a meal is a welcome gesture. But generous words are one thing. National action is something else. Over the past few years, I'm afraid, we've seen a lot more of the former than the latter. Military veterans cannot live by back pats alone. I'd trade some of those for some meaningful action.

We demanded so much from these willing warriors. We sent them into some God-awful war zones. We asked them to risk their lives for us. No one can say yet when this war on terrorism will end. The various missions are constantly debated. But whatever the purpose was, the troops did what we asked them to, every mile of the journey. Great nations have to act in great ways, and when it comes to the treatment of our post-9/11 military, we still have far to go.

WORLD WAR II: THE HIGH POINT

This is one issue where we can learn a lot from the past, seeing what succeeded—and, just as important, what failed. World War II was the gold standard for how America welcomed its troops home from war. Most people felt good about how the war ended. Everyone loved the veterans. War heroes were everywhere. I wasn't around then, but I've read and heard enough stories from my older relatives and others who experienced it firsthand. Alfred Eisenstaedt's famous *Life* magazine photo—the sailor exuberantly kissing the nurse on V-J Day in Times Square—sums up the mood I am talking about. And the nation's support went far beyond handshakes, free beers at the local tavern, and kisses from pretty nurses. The nation and its leaders unfurled a massive program of benefits for returning veterans that far surpassed anything that had been enacted before.

The official name was the Servicemen's Readjustment Act of 1944, but everyone called it the GI Bill. It was a life-changing and nation-changing enterprise. The GI Bill had many facets: low-interest mortgages for buying a home; inexpensive loans for starting a business; cash for tuition and living expenses for college, graduate school, or technical training; a full year of unemployment benefits.

In the 1920s and 1930s, the confusing mishmash of programs for returning World War I soldiers had turned into a political and bureaucratic mess. Relatively few veterans received meaningful assistance and no one was happy with the results. As World War II was coming to an end, Republicans and Democrats both vowed to do a better job and not to make the same mistakes. They lived up to the promise—the GI Bill was a smashing political and economic success. America was truly reshaped by it.

The GI Bill made higher education a reality for millions of everyday Americans, quickly giving the nation the best-trained workforce on earth. It turned home ownership into a core value of the American Dream, helping to build the modern suburbs. The GI Bill launched an unprecedented boom in entrepreneurship as thousands of new businesses were started. Without the GI Bill, it's hard to imagine the modern American middle class. An expanding economy, the first real glimmers of an ownership society, better-trained workers, steadily growing demand. Perhaps it's an exaggeration to say the GI Bill did all this—but not too much of an exaggeration. From 1944 to 1949, nearly nine million veterans received close to $4 billion in unemployment checks. By 1956, 2.2 million veterans had used the GI Bill's education benefits to attend universities and another 5.6 million to attend technical schools. And the benefits lasted well past the immediate postwar years. The education and training provisions were extended until 1956. The low-cost mortgages continued into the early 1960s. They totaled more than $50 billion. Various benefits of the GI Bill were eventually extended to veterans of the Korean War and—with the Readjustment Benefits Act of 1966—to all military veterans, including those who had served during peacetime.

In the course of American history, you'd be hard-pressed to find a government program, with the possible exception of Social Security, with as dramatic an effect on the lives of so many.

If we could do all that for World War II veterans and leave the nation so much better off, there's no reason we can't do something similar again. Vietnam gave us a chilling example of what to avoid.

VIETNAM: THE LOW POINT

It wasn't just that some aspects of the GI Bill were getting ready to expire, though they were. It wasn't just that veterans' benefits were somewhat stingier in the Vietnam years either, though that was also true. It was something more profound. It was that the nation's attitude toward the conflict and those who went to war dramatically changed.

In the late 1960s, more than 90 percent of the country had television sets. For the first time in history, nightly television brought vivid reports of deadly encounters, burned villages, and dead children into the homes of all Americans. The ground war had proven far more difficult than anyone expected. The Viet Cong and the North Vietnamese regulars hadn't succumbed like they were supposed to. Americans grew frustrated with the seeming lack of success.

In fact, many of our troops performed spectacularly in Vietnam. In Ap Bac, the Ia Drang Valley, Khe Sanh, and other corners of the jungle most Americans had never heard of, they learned an entirely new style of warfare. Our special operators, especially, came into their own there, including Underwater Demolition Teams from the Navy who were reconstituted into an elite, antiguerrilla force proficient on the sea, in the air, and on the land. SEALs, these fighters were called, but most Americans weren't interested in hearing about that. As eyewitnesses through the lenses of reporters, Americans felt more deeply connected to the war and were more apt to have negative emotions about it.

The protests and politics at home grew increasingly acrimonious as the war dragged on, not just against the war but against the troops who served. In some people's eyes, the lowliest grunt bore the same responsibility as President Johnson or General Westmoreland. Because of this, as large numbers of troops returned to American soil, many of their fellow citizens hated everything about the war, including the men and women who fought it. The veterans grew to symbolize a war that was highly unpopular and that many Americans objected to on moral grounds. Many faced hostile comments on the street. "Baby killers," they were called, and "American imperialists." What was especially maddening was that many of them hadn't chosen to go in the first place—they were drafted. They certainly didn't set the policies that sent them to fight. Rarely were any of these distinctions made.

The hostility toward the Vietnam veterans was a breach of a national trust that I can hardly wrap my head around. Those troops came home the same way World War II veterans did, the same way my buddies and I returned from Iraq and Afghanistan. And yet the way they were treated could not have been more upside down.

Our government asked its citizens to go to Vietnam—

even drafting many of them—and when they returned home, they were spat on for leaving in the first place. The message was horrendous—an act of sheer cruelty. It was bound to mess our guys up. And it did. So this is why I still see guys on American street corners in canvas fatigue jackets panhandling from cars at red lights. I don't think all of them are Vietnam veterans—some just claim they are for sympathy, but a lot of these people did serve in the Vietnam War, doing what we asked of them, and they are still paying the price. Some who came out of the Vietnam War are severely damaged. The national attitude toward veterans during this time makes me ill to think about, even now. These men and women risked their lives—and that was the thanks they got.

GIVE OUR VETS WHAT THEY REALLY NEED

Clearly, we are doing much better now in our treatment of returning veterans, on a personal level at least. "Thank you for your service" has probably been said a billion times by now. So why are things only a little better for today's generation of veterans? What's still lacking? How can we get this right once and for all?

It's not that the recent wars we've been involved in were overwhelmingly popular. There was public opposition to the conflicts in Afghanistan and Iraq—plenty of it. But it was never quite as virulent as the anger Vietnam generated. And there's been no draft to fuel whatever outrage is simmering.

Some of the improvement, I believe, can be traced to a quiet, national soul-searching that has occurred since the end of the Vietnam War. People reflected on how shabbily those vets were treated and swore, "Never again." No one, regardless of politics or persuasion, could be comfortable with how things went the last time. Almost everyone recognized the cruelty and dreadfulness. That's a positive trait of everyday Americans, the ability to learn from experience and make better judgments the next time around. The warmer welcome for the post-9/11 warriors is an excellent example.

One other factor goes into it as well, I am convinced. I wouldn't call it guilt exactly. It's more like recognition, spiced with a sigh of relief. Recognition that a small coterie of Americans were carrying everyone's burden in these recent wars. Relief that these rare individuals were willing to go. Given that reality, a friendly gesture in an airport feels like a very small price to pay.

People also seem to have a more acute understanding today of what it means to serve. When they see someone in uniform these days, Americans know that, chances are, that person has been somewhere pretty dicey—facing down real bad guys—and is fortunate to be coming home alive. Only someone truly heartless could be ungrateful for that.

But still, we owe them more than a pat on the back.

The way we treat today's generation of veterans has to flow directly from the unique way they have served. Today's military keeps being asked to do more. The reach and capability of the U.S. military has never been greater than it is right now. Our talented personnel, our focused command, our high-tech wizardry—together, they've vastly expanded the power of any individual warrior. At the same time, we are not just a fighting force anymore. We're a rebuilding force. A social-development force. A democracy-in-training force. We are handed missions far beyond what militaries have traditionally done, which was capturing and holding pieces of territory long enough for political authority to settle in.

No one was drafted into today's all-volunteer force, but it's not like all recent recruits were itching to get into battle. Many enlisted for the reasons military recruits always have—for training and opportunity, to see the world, to get away from tough big cities or boring small towns. Many of them signed up for the National Guard or the Reserves, not expecting combat. "We're going to pay for your school," the recruiter told them. "Two days a month, two weeks a year. Come out and play GI Joe. Piece of cake. It'll be fun." The next thing these men and women knew, they were in a Humvee or an MRAP, speeding down a highway seeded with IEDs and holding on for dear life. Then one deployment turned into two or three—and no one could honestly promise when it would end. It was a truly harrowing experience for many of these volunteers.

These men and women were also called upon to serve longer than veterans in any other time in our history. We sent these young pups away from their families for indefensibly large blocks of time. America suffered huge casualties in World War II and Vietnam. But most people who went to Vietnam were there for a year. Of the relative few who re-upped, most of them completed two or three tours max. In World War II, many deployments were for the duration of the war, but not all. Many troops came home after a year, and that war didn't last nearly as long as those in Iraq and Afghanistan.

Soldiers were sent back to Iraq and Afghanistan for five, six, seven, eight, nine, even double-digit deployments. I believe in the job. It's been a defining part of my life. I get it. And every soldier thinks his war was the toughest. But some of those deployments were for as long as eighteen months. We've never in our nation's military history seen anything like this before. What's the cumulative toll from all these repeat deployments? With no historical precedent, we are only now finding out, and little of it's pretty.

At the Pentagon, the multiple deployments in Afghanistan and Iraq were tempting from a managerial point of view. We had the bodies uniformed, trained, and ready—why not keep sending them back out? And generally speaking, an experienced soldier is a more capable soldier. But I'm sorry, that's just criminal. Eighteen months in combat zones as hot as these places. Eighteen months without seeing your family and friends. The emotional impact is excruciating, even if you do come home alive. What we've seen with multiple hard redeployments is not right. Whatever we do in the future, we must take a different course.

Thankfully, as Iraq and Afghanistan were winding down, some overdue changes were made in deployment rules. They differed from service to service, but a growing recognition took hold among the top commanders that there are limits to what the human body and the mind can absorb.

At last.

In my world, new standards were finally put in place by the Special Operations Command, calling for a finite number of days that our troops are allowed to go out without coming home. The command decided any more than that is unhealthy. The previous standards were counterproductive and wrong.

This generation of veterans did what we trained them to. They came home, and things started to fall apart. We have an utterly inadequate system for curing the damage war has done to them. As their friends, neighbors, and strangers on the street told the veterans how appreciated they are, many of the government programs designed to help them kept coming up dramatically short. We built the on-ramp very effectively, but we can't seem to build a comparable off-ramp for these people we've brought in.

At its core, it's a problem of national resources and bureaucratic commitment—too little money for too big a job at too tough a time. The overall number of people hurt but not killed in Iraq and Afghanistan is maddeningly hard to pin down. The best estimates run around one million nonfatal casualties, and that doesn't include everyone, just those who have sought treatment at military and VA hospitals and clinics for Iraq or Afghanistan war injuries. We know that, overall, 2.6 million medical and disability claims have already been made. The conditions treated include everything from minor ailments to lost limbs, serious burns, loss of sight and hearing, and traumatic brain injuries. In earlier wars, many of these people wouldn't have survived. The talented, overworked medical professionals deserve great credit for this. But both recent wars have left us with a great number of people in need of long-term, serious medical treatment and care.

For some people, like many of my SEAL buddies and me, you can point to how badly we got banged up by the large amount of action we've seen. The number of times we hit the ground at a high rate of speed; jumped off a Humvee when it was moving; had concussive explosions in and around us; the wear and tear on joints, ankles, hips, backs, shoulders, and multiple surgeries—it all added up over the years. And it was all done in service to our country. At a minimum, I think our guys should get an automatic 50 percent disability.

I don't consider myself a disabled veteran, but my body will definitely hit the wall at some point and cry out in pain: "You weren't as good to me as you could have been." That said, I don't complain about it. I knew exactly what I was signing up for. Frankly, I sought it out. But the system for dealing with even these relatively minor cases really isn't in place yet, even as the wars that caused them are largely complete.

We take on a sacred moral duty when we send troops off to war. The nation has to patch them back together and ease them on their way. We have to make them whole again. Don't send our young men and women to war unless you are willing to shoulder that.

I don't want to blame the Department of Veterans Affairs for everything. A lot of good-intentioned people are working their tails off there. But if you told me tomorrow we could dissolve the VA, I have to believe we could create some other kind of health-and-welfare system to care for our veterans more effectively, more efficiently, and with fewer deadly mistakes.

Despite plenty of good intentions, we aren't close to getting where we need to be. Long waits for doctor visits. Too much substandard treatment—far too little psychological care. I am very concerned about what this might mean in the long run, the physical and, especially, the psychological tolls. These are going to be big issues for the next five or six decades. That's no exaggeration. We're going to see some very disturbing cases in the years to come and we'd better be ready for it. We are only now learning how much damage has been done. There is a cumulative pounding—emotional, psychological, and physical—that comes with all these multiple deployments. There really is a point where the body and mind can't take any more, even if the soldier doesn't realize it.

We can't underestimate the psychological trauma of it all.

A key part of the SEAL training and culture is the ability to absorb and metabolize suffering and pain. Sadly, what makes us effective on the battlefield also leaves some of our teammates ill-prepared to ease back into civilian life. They don't quickly recognize or communicate the lingering issues they may have. They are slow to seek help. I have plenty of friends who suffered too long in silence—experiencing intense emotional trauma—not realizing the assistance that was available to them.

For too long, people in and out of the military saw these

psychological traumas of war as signs of personal weakness. Those who were brave enough to admit they'd suffered psychological damage were considered shameful, abnormal, and disgraceful. Injuries to the mind suggested a lack of courage or masculinity, or at the very least an inability to cope with stress. This ignorant view carried terrible consequences, burdening the lives of many decent soldiers. The message to them: shut up and tough it out. It became clear that seeking help—even acknowledging an issue—could slam the brakes on a promising military career. So people hid these struggles from their buddies, commanders, families, and even from themselves.

Fortunately, we are smarter now and much more open to recognizing these unseen wounds of war. The military now does a better job of confronting this than in the old days. There is far more internal recognition and public acceptance of PTSD that often rattles combat veterans. These are the wounds of war that are by far the hardest to heal. I have learned a lot from Dr. Eric Potterat, a clinical psychologist who has worked closely with the SEAL teams. His central insight: PTSD isn't a sign of weakness or insanity. It is a normal reaction to abnormal events. We should never harshly judge those who are bravely confronting it.

The studies involving the military and war's psychological toll are mostly unreliable and incomplete. But we do know some things. We know the numbers are large, and these wounds can be naggingly slow to heal. No one really knows the full extent of the problem. There is still too much stigma surrounding these issues.

Twenty-two a day.

That's how many military veterans have been killing themselves, according to a national estimate based on a Department of Veterans Affairs analysis of death records from twenty-one states.

Twenty-two a day. Let me repeat that number. It's just so shocking; it's hard to get my head around. The first time I heard that number, I was literally shaken by it. I wondered if it could really be true. That's more than 650 soldier suicides in a month's time. More than 8,000 veterans in a year.

With numbers so large, you would think we could simply learn which ones are most susceptible and provide help. But there is no one single cause. It is not just people who have seen the most intense combat. It's not easy to predict in advance who is most vulnerable. But I'm convinced these multiple deployments must play a role.

That twenty-two-a-day figure isn't just Iraq and Afghanistan veterans. It includes veterans from other wars, but it clearly illustrates how serious a mental-health epidemic we have on our hands. Another recent study found the suicide rates were highest during the first three years out of the military. This obviously requires much more study and far more concerted action on the government's part. Some research from top hospitals and universities might help too. We still don't know nearly enough about the causes or the cures. We just know how deadly real this issue is.

War keeps kicking back at us, like the recoil of a powerful rifle. The suicide rate is too high, but there are many other ways that a tormented mind can snap. I think about some of today's mass civilian shootings where someone loses it at a school, a movie theater, or a shopping mall. Most often these crazed perpetrators have practiced on video games, gotten their hands on a weapon, and stockpiled a cache of ammunition. Then their deranged scenario turned deadly real.

But what if the next gunman turned out to be a military-trained special operator or someone else with extensive battle experience? What happens if the next sniper is actually a sniper? If someone like that snaps, he could effectively hit every target he takes a shot at, eliminating multiple moving targets one by one. He'd know how to evade the counterforce of civilian authorities and could commit an awful lot of carnage in a very short time. And what happens when the explosives come out?

If you need another reason to support expanded mental-health treatment for war veterans, that's not a bad one.

We've waited long enough. Now is the time for fresh action from our government and those who pay the bills: make high-quality physical- and mental-health treatment readily available. Destigmatize the need for treatment. Train veterans for better jobs. Hire them to do the kinds of jobs they are now capable of. Fairness demands it. Decency demands it. So does our own national self-interest. These vets can be tremendously valuable members of society.

TRIDENT TAKEAWAYS

- War always takes its toll.
- More like World War II, less like Vietnam.
- Treat vets right.

CHAPTER 10

UNITED WE STAND

We weren't there just to kill people. Like many U.S. military units in Iraq, my SEAL team and I were also expected to help the Iraqi people live together in something approaching peace. Nation-building, some people called this, but in many ways, Iraq was hardly a nation at all.

When I arrived in Iraq, I remembered the stories my father read to my brother and me when we were boys. Human civilization literally grew up there more than eight thousand years ago. The area between the Tigris and Euphrates Rivers was the very first place where people learned to read, write, live in cities, establish laws, and accept civil government. I'd studied all this in school, and I was excited to be part of any effort to rescue such a special place.

Recent history had not been so kind. Iraq didn't spring

naturally into nationhood. The country was cobbled together by British mapmakers and the League of Nations. The modern borders were set in 1920 when the Ottoman Empire was divided by the Treaty of Sèvres—Turkey to the north, Syria to the west, Jordan to the southwest, Saudi Arabia to the south, Kuwait to the southeast, and Iran to the east. A new entity known as the British Mandate of Mesopotamia was placed under the authority of the United Kingdom, and the Brits were immediately perplexed by it. A monarchy was established in 1921 and the Kingdom of Iraq gained independence eleven years later. Twenty-six years after that, the monarchy was toppled, and the Republic of Iraq was born.

Throughout this period, people of this made-up country never really thought of themselves as one. They were Arabs and Kurds, Sunni and Shia, Assyrians, Turkmen, Shabakis, Annenians, Mandeans, Circassians, and Kawlinya—far more intensely than they were Iraqis. It took a pair of strong-willed leaders from the Arab Socialist Ba'ath Party—despotic dictators, really—to hold this accidental country together. Ahmed Hassan al-Bakr and Saddam Hussein were both unblinking in their brutality and dedicated to their own megalomania. Once Saddam was ousted after the U.S. invasion in 2003, only massive American troop strength could keep Iraq from coming unglued.

Our American forces were supplemented with local Iraqi

soldiers, who we trained and integrated into our teams. They were a very mixed bag. Many developed into competent and dedicated warriors, and we were happy to have them. Some were uninterested, undisciplined, and not to be trusted. We got rid of the bad ones as quickly as we could. But even those assignments—which Iraqi soldiers got sent where—had to take into account the fractured realities of the nation of Iraq. If you were from Ramadi, you would not operate in Ramadi. You might get sent to Mosul. If you were from Mosul, you might go to Tikrit. Those were almost different countries as far as the Iraqis were concerned.

The policy was understandable. It could be uncomfortable for an Iraqi soldier, fighting against his own cousin, neighbor, or classmate from school. There could be reprisals against his family if he was recognized. On the other hand, we did occasionally get local people assigned to us, and their knowledge of the area was a huge asset. They knew the rhythms. They knew who was who. They could walk down a block and say, "Good house, bad house. Bad house, good house," helping us pinpoint where to target our attention. A guy from another Iraqi province didn't know those neighborhoods any better than we did.

When I got to Afghanistan in 2007, that country was, if anything, even more fractured than Iraq. In Afghanistan, the divisions weren't based so much on broad regional differences or competing ethnicities. Ancient tribalism was much more at play. The tribalism here was often literal, defined by tribes. Village against village. Clan against clan. Warlord against warlord. There was no faction so small in Afghanistan that its leaders couldn't find another faction to clash with. The one thing that brought them together, it seemed, was their shared disdain for "invaders" and, especially, "occupiers."

Afghanistan is a landlocked nation of only thirty-one million people. They are jammed between Pakistan, Iran, Turkmenistan, Uzbekistan, Tajikistan, and China. The largest cash crop is the poppy, which can be processed into heroin. The people here have been fighting—against outsiders and against one another—for millennia. Kushans, Hephthalites, Samanids, Saffarids, Ghaznavids, Ghorids, Mughals, Hotaks, and Durranis all rose from this rugged terrain to form empires. And long before the modern Western powers arrived, Alexander the Great, Muslim Arabs, Mongols, the British, and, more recently, the Soviets all tried and failed to dominate this land.

It wasn't by accident that Afghanistan became known as "the graveyard of empires." Those outside powers all failed to appreciate that the local people were every bit as rugged as the terrain. However much the Afghanis might bicker with one another, they hated outsiders ten times more. The nation was so sufficiently lawless and factionalized that the architects

of 9/11 found Afghanistan an ideal place to train and orga-
nize their evil plans.

In Afghanistan, every single valley seemed to have its own
fortress, its own warlord, its own clan and elders in charge.
Their blood feuds went back centuries and seemed unlikely
to ever end. Given half a chance, these people would gladly
wipe one another off the face of the planet. I'll give just one
firsthand example. Two neighboring tribes were from different family bloodlines but had coexisted in the same valley for
hundreds and hundreds of years. Elders from the two tribes
were disputing control of a field that both sides wanted for
poppies. As neutral outside arbitrators, we were trying to help
settle their disagreement.

There was no discussion of legal titles, land records, or
experts weighing in. There was no local courthouse where the
two elders could take their real-estate quarrel. Before resort-
ing to violence, the men met face-to-face one last time to
cajole, to argue, to threaten and plead. To me, that sounded
promising, modern almost, attempting to negotiate a reso-
lution to a long-simmering dispute. But then I learned one
other detail that seemed to catapult the process back to a
time far before modern diplomacy. It felt as if we were back
in the fifth century.

Before one of the tribal leaders left his house that morning, he took both his shoes off. He grabbed a handful of dirt

from outside his house and poured the dirt into his left shoe. Then he took another handful and emptied it into his right shoe. The other tribal leader, at his own house, did exactly the same thing. I didn't see them do this, but our interpreter explained it to me later.

"That way," the interpreter said, "they can both honestly say to their family and their god that wherever they walk in that disputed field, they are standing on their own ground."

That was for real.

To a casual observer, it might sound like a small, harmless ritual. On one level, I suppose it was. But to me, it symbolized so much about Afghanistan and its ancient factions. I recognized that all the logic and discussion in the world was unlikely to bridge the ancient divides.

We were there pushing to make improvements, bridge long-standing divisions. But as we tried to figure out how to manage these people and their behaviors, it was flashes like these rituals that eventually made all of us understand: we're a long way from home and a long way from the twenty-first century.

Spending time in Iraq and Afghanistan made clear to me what can happen when the divisions within a society are so sharp and so deep it's almost impossible to ease them.

Back home in America, we don't have tribes like they do in those two countries, thank God. But that doesn't mean we don't have our own version of tribes. We have our divisions, our own narrow-mindedness, our own high walls, and they don't always serve us well. I believe we are in a place where the differences we have could cause genuine problems moving forward. The flashpoints between the races. The sharp separation between the red and blue states. The utter inability of today's politicians to reach across the aisle and get important work done.

Our own domestic tribal differences have devolved into major challenges, and all the pointed talk in the media doesn't help. The rhetoric of politics and government has grown so harsh and personal it can be almost impossible to find common ground. We aren't facing off yet with armed warlords. But too often we shrug and accept our dysfunctional divisions as normal.

This has to stop. There are several clear steps we can take to be sure it does.

OPEN YOUR MIND TO NEW IDEAS
AND START THINKING FOR YOURSELF

It is far too easy in America today to surround ourselves with people who are pretty much the same as we are. We live in a hugely diverse country with people from every background, religion, nationality, class, and cultural attitude. And yet we still tend to stick with those who look like we do and think like we do. I get it. Lions hang out with lions. Zebras hang out with zebras. And proximity does not always equal tolerance or understanding. The news media makes this instinct to stay in our comfort zones worse by catering to one outlook or another. Conservatives watch Fox, liberals listen to NPR. Many young people don't consume any news at all. For the first time in American history, it is possible now to go all day and night without ever hearing a contrary point of view. That's not healthy, especially in a nation as diverse as this one.

A lot of our divisions, I have noticed, are fueled by politicians and the media, who fan people's worst instincts and prejudices. These cynical players have learned how to divide by race, color, creed, wealth, gender identity, and sexual orientation—all for their own benefit. Stirring resentment against the successful or hostility toward the poor. Making liberals hate conservatives, and pushing conservatives to return the favor. There are votes to be captured and ratings to be earned by keeping people apart. The last thing the panderers want to see is large numbers of diverse Americans realizing how much we have in common, after all.

This is disgraceful. It is damaging to our society. It undermines our national ability to solve our problems together. It ought to be called out publicly every time it occurs.

At heart, most Americans aren't hard-core ideologues, one-hundred-percent-down-the-line anything. Most of us are more individual and interesting than that. We'd rather think for ourselves. That's certainly true of most people I know. They are conservative about some things, liberal about others, and downright radical or totally apathetic about a few stray issues. Despite the easy slogans about "red" and "blue" America, I think most real people share opinions with both sides. But we all need to work extra hard to keep our minds open.

I know who I like reading and listening to in the media. I have several columnists, commentators, and radio talk-show hosts whose work I respect, enjoy, and often learn from. There are certain newspapers and magazines I find myself drawn to, in large part because they see the world pretty much as I do. My thinking has been immeasurably enriched by the great minds of people like Hugh Hewitt, Dennis Prager, Victor Davis Hanson, and Mark Steyn. Those are some of the thought leaders I've followed for years. But if I take an honest look at that lineup, I have to admit there is not a lot of diversity there. It is all pretty much one voice. When I think about it, I can see there is something psychologically pleasing about reading or listening to a smart person articulate opinions you already have. It's hard to resist the feeling of "I must be right. Look at all the brilliant thinkers who agree with me."

I've learned that I benefit from hearing things I disagree with, even if I don't always enjoy it. It challenges me and stretches my mind. So I make a point of tuning into NPR or catching up with the essays on Salon.com or in the *Guardian*. All of us, me included, would do well to broaden the input a little and seek out perspectives different from our own. Find the best and brightest on the other side. The people who start with premises or priorities that are different from our own—and explore them with interest.

If you spend all day with people who think and act exactly like you do, you just constantly reinforce one another's narrow beliefs.

"Good point."

"I agree."

"You are absolutely correct, sir."

That's no way to expand your worldview.

One of my closest friends is hyperbright with highly liberal political views. James is a self-described Prius-driving, kale-growing resident of the "socialist workers paradise of Vermont." His words. I suppose his views are considered middle-of-the-road there. We talk about all sorts of things—politics, religion, social trends, movies, and sports. On many fundamental issues, we are north- and southbound trains. If we put copies of our voting records side by side, very few boxes would overlap. But to write off half the nation because of political leanings seems both shortsighted and intellectually limiting to me. By keeping the conversation going—in spite of our differences—James and I learned that we agree on the elemental stuff. We are loyal patriots and hard-line First Amendment absolutists. We judge other people on their actions and character. We would never fail to help a friend or sacrifice everything for our families.

James is one of the most interesting people I ever get to talk to—and part of the reason is that we look at the world so differently. He challenges many of my strongly held opinions, and I challenge his. We respect each other. We like each other. We just think differently. That keeps things interesting and fun. My conversations with James are some of the best I've ever had.

Diversity of relationships is actually one of the special advantages of being in the military. People come from all over with different backgrounds, different life experiences, and all kinds of different attitudes. We are thrown together and expected to work as one. Even public high school doesn't quite deliver that. It's all God's creatures in the military, blended together.

There is always another side. And don't tell me, "There are no smart people over there. All the smart people agree with me." That's almost proof that you have closed your mind to new ideas. This doesn't mean you have to give up your own principles. In fact, your principles will often be strengthened as you bounce them against the heartfelt principles of others. There is no doubt about it.

IGNORE CASTE SYSTEMS—RANK, TITLE, FAME, AND WEALTH

The myth that it is no longer possible to achieve social mobility is another factor that creates division in America. Reject that idea. I have no doubt that if you were born in Darien, Connecticut, or Winnetka, Illinois, or Great Neck, New York, and have parents who both went to Ivy League colleges and you attended an exclusive prep school, you have some genuine advantages over people who did not. And if you were raised in Compton, California, or the South Side of Chicago, or in some desolate hollow in the hills of Appalachia with seven brothers and sisters and a struggling single mom, you are very differently prepared for getting to a better place in life. We still have racial differences, class differences, educational differences, and geographical differences. All those things are real. Equality of opportunity is something we are moving toward, not something we have fully achieved in America.

That being said, the idea of equal opportunity and the

possibility for upward mobility go all the way back to the American Revolution. "All men are created equal," Thomas Jefferson wrote without any equivocation at all.

Jefferson crafted that immortal phrase and used it first in the Declaration of Independence. It was one of the rallying cries of the revolution and has been at the core of the American ideal ever since. And who could disagree with the distinguished historian Jack P. Greene? "Perhaps no single phrase from the Revolutionary era has had such continuing importance in American public life as the dictum 'all men are created equal.'"

Jefferson didn't dream it up entirely on his own. Some say he was inspired by the writings of his friend and Virginia neighbor, Philip Mazzei, an Italian-born patriot and pamphleteer. Jefferson certainly got a powerful assist from Thomas Payne's sensational "Common Sense," which appeared in January 1776. "All men are by nature equally free and independent," Payne wrote anonymously, helping to provoke a revolutionary fervor across the thirteen colonies. "Such equality is necessary in order to create a free government. All men must be equal to one another in natural law."

While Jefferson's notion of "men" has certainly expanded over the centuries—neither women nor African slaves were on his list—his idea of equality went far beyond the politics or sociology of the eighteenth-century world. He tied equality straight to God. This right wasn't just wrestled away from far-off monarchs or grabbed by men with muskets. It was God-given, inherent in our humanity, and could not legitimately be taken away.

In Jefferson's mind, this was always an equality of opportunity, not of result. Other, competing rights made sure of that. The pursuit of happiness by free individuals, another core concept, would inevitably produce unequal results, he believed. Some people would be more talented than others. Some would work harder. But God had created all men equal, Jefferson was certain, and that idea has been with us, albeit imperfectly, ever since. It's at the very foundation of our legal system. It has served us well for nearly two and a half centuries now. It's a core plank in how Americans see themselves and how we are seen around the world.

There is nothing to match this anywhere else on earth.

While you might hear something different through the media, today the whole structure of American society is designed to let people get ahead. No, it's not easy. In fact it's hard. But upward mobility is far from impossible today, and I have irrefutable proof: many of the people I know who have achieved it, both men and women, come from some of the toughest corners of America. There are few things more inspiring and encouraging than seeing people you care about bettering their lives and the lives of their families.

Tell me the odds are far from certain. That's undeniable. Tell me some people have an easier time than others. No doubt. But do not tell me that social advance is just a myth or a dream in America. I will gladly introduce you to some of my friends.

Meet A.J. He was born in Trinidad and immigrated to America when he was twelve years old. After struggling mightily in school, he was a bar bouncer, a laborer, and Muay Thai fighter before he joined the SEAL teams, becoming an absolutely standout performer of ours.

Meet Ed, whose father was a welder in small-town Colorado and died even before the boy reached his teens. After school, Ed spent a dozen years as a junior gear rep for a major outdoors company. One day he said: "I could do all this by starting my own company," and he did. Now he runs regional sales and marketing for his old employers and spends his off time on a top-of-the-line fishing boat that he docks near his beach house in Cabo San Lucas, Mexico.

And meet David. He was raised in a violent, abusive household. His stepfather was murdered when David was five years old. One of the few African American students in his school, he battled obesity, allergies, sickle cell, and a congenital heart defect. He let none of that slow him down. He joined the SEALs and went on to become a competitive ultramarathon runner, whose fitness feats include the world record for most pull-ups in a single twenty-four-hour period.

It *should* all start at home with parents who care, but it really takes off in school. One of the great things about America is that we have a free public-education system that makes learning available to everyone. Literally, everyone. Anyone, in any place, of any ability. We have training and enrichment programs open to anyone who is willing to show up and do the work. We have scholarships, mentors, and other pathways to success. What we don't have is anyone who will do the work for you. You're on your own there. But the ladder is waiting, and I swear it is pointing toward the stars. If you apply yourself and start climbing, you can really get somewhere.

Our country is large enough, secure enough, diverse enough, wealthy enough, and blessed enough to deliver on that promise. In many different fields, especially the military, we need dedicated, hardworking people who will throw themselves into things. And when they do, our economy is able to reward those efforts.

It's a mathematical fact: the upper 1 percent only has room for 1 percent. Even there, the membership ebbs and flows. Bill Gates, Warren Buffett, and Larry Ellison are probably safe for a while at the very top. But a rung or two beneath them, others are constantly climbing up or slipping down. Some new tech wiz is shooting into the stratosphere while a one-hit-wonder entertainer is diving fast. In that thin atmosphere, you really do need a program to keep the top players straight.

If you are like most Americans and you were born somewhere in the vast middle—or even at the lower end—your effort is still rewarded, almost as much as your talent. It may not always feel that way. But none of us in America are so low that we can't start pulling ourselves up.

A little perspective is always helpful, a frank assessment of what deprivation means in America and elsewhere. We talk about the poor in this country, the haves and the have-nots. That's a reality. But compared to the poor in a lot of places, most of the have-nots here still have it pretty darned good. Go to the most distressed parts of our country. Ask a couple of questions. Make an honest assessment of what you see. I have talked to some of my buddies who came from very rough towns and neighborhoods. I don't want to downplay how hard they have struggled, but in most homes in America, even in the lowest-income areas, people still have decent shelter, modern kitchen appliances, and flat-screen TVs. The vast majority of people, even in the most downtrodden areas, have cell phones and cars.

Compare that to India, the world's largest democracy.

People picking rags to eke out a living. People living in tumbledown corrugated shacks without electricity, flush toilets, or clean water. People trying to support families on less than a dollar a day. That is poor.

That's not to ignore that great imbalances still exist in our country. But they are far less severe than in many places—African dictatorships, oil-rich kingdoms of the Middle East, or nations like Russia, where the superrich can be counted on the fingers of two hands. For most people in those places, there really is no way up. When the old Soviet Union collapsed, all the old cronies saw the social disorder as a ripe opportunity to deal out the spoils like a hand of cards. "Okay, you take gas and oil. You take power. You take finance." Those are real oligarchies, where the vast, vast majority of people are simply shut out. In America, every door may not always be open. But with sufficient drive and motivation, most of them can still be mule-kicked in.

That's why it irritates me so much when people just accept their station in life. Even more, it bothers me when people use where they started as an excuse not to achieve. Grab every opportunity. Refuse to accept your station in life if you are unsatisfied. Accept no limitations on ambition, especially your own. Sometimes, the highest walls are the ones we build inside our minds, accepting where we are and limiting how far we can imagine going. Don't do that. I am always inspired by people who choose to ignore those supposed limitations.

Abraham Lincoln was born in a log cabin with dirt floors, learning to read by candlelight. He did pretty well, don't you think? Teddy Roosevelt was a sickly child who grew into a rough-riding man-beast and a world-class outdoorsman. He also had a nice political career. Frederick Douglass went from escaped slave to writer, orator, rights crusader, abolitionist leader, and statesman because he wouldn't accept anyone's limitation of what he could do. When plantation owners argued that slaves lacked the intellectual capacity to be free, all Douglass had to do was begin to speak. No one could deny his brilliance. Too-small linebacker Pat Tillman wasn't supposed to make his high school football team, his college football team, or his NFL team, until he did. American history is replete with uplifting examples like these.

Let's not kid ourselves. The United States has work to do if we are going to live up to the ideal Mazzei, Payne, and Jefferson articulated as a standard we can all be proud of today. Democracy and opportunity are concepts that need to be constantly nourished. We are reminded of our shortcomings in this regard almost every day. People are struggling out there. A mom and two kids are abandoned by a father. A middle-aged construction worker is unemployed again. A police officer shoots an unarmed teenager, and a whole city erupts. A young college graduate, saddled with student loans, is having a terrible time landing a job in her chosen career. Where one salary used to support a family, it now takes two and a half. Housing is expensive.

The internal differences in America are real and not easy to bridge. New York City and rural Idaho are sufficiently different from each other that sometimes they really do feel like they could be separate countries. It's not just urban-rural, liberal-conservative, Democratic-Republican. It's those things and more. It's almost everything. Attitudes about faith and religion. The whole notion of community. Very different views about the role of government.

This shouldn't be surprising. The people in different parts of America live very differently. So, of course, they will come at some issues from a different perspective. Does that mean that as a country we will have real trouble coming together when we need to? No! Remember 9/11? Everyone does. And what is most memorable about that terrible experience, besides the tragic loss of human life, was how the nation and much of the outside world came together in grief, outrage, and sympathy. September 11 was a notable bonding moment.

The spirit of oneness has dissipated over time. But the seeds for unity as a country exist. We need to nurture them.

TRIDENT TAKEAWAYS

➤ Build your own ladder of upward mobility.

➤ Don't let anyone narrow your dreams.

➤ Take strength from like-minded allies,
but open your mind to people with other
points of view.

ONWARD

The call is sounded again.

My call came from Winston Churchill my senior year in college. Yours will likely come from someone else.

If you take anything away from this book, let it be the importance and joy of serving, doing your part to help make this glorious country of ours better every day. Never before have the opportunities been more plentiful. Never before have the challenges been more daunting, especially the self-inflicted ones.

Freedom tastes sweeter to those who have struggled to secure it—especially to those who have sacrificed their comfort, their safety, their time, and their creativity to causes larger than themselves. My own deep appreciation for America flows from the challenges I have shouldered on her behalf. In the SEAL teams, I found my vehicle for life-changing service. That's a fine one, and there are thousands of others. Service, in the military and elsewhere, always leaves that special taste.

We as a nation are generously blessed with heroes. There are many worth looking up to and learning from. I have shared my own personal list. After reflecting on what you consider most important, you can assemble a list of your own. Follow the lessons these people teach.

Live boldly. Act decisively. Stand for something real. The people who built our country did that. We must too. Jump in and behave according to the highest standards you have set for yourself. That is what the spirit of America teaches us. Pursue the happiness that is the reward for those who serve others. Pass it on. Be that person others will look up to. Be a hero.

ACKNOWLEDGMENTS

Far too often, I find, more is favored over enough. But when it comes to giving thanks, I'm all for going overboard. That may be because I have so many people who deserve to be thanked. All I can say is I've tried to keep this as tight and concise as I can. Here goes:

To my family: You are my forever fuel. You are also the spark that ignites that fuel into action. On this effort, my dad and my brother, Nate, had valuable edits and artistic direction for every chapter. My bride was peerless in her copyediting and kept helping me find words that better described what I thought.

To Ellis, a friend before cowriter, a thinker, fighter, comic, and plow horse. I will miss cranking out chapters until we do it again! Special nod to Janis, Roberta, and James.

To my reps at Foundry, Brillstein, and Ziffren Brittenham: Aces all. Let's stay in the hunt.

To the folks at Howard Books: I am humbled by the faith, better for the effort, appreciative of the diligence, and excited for more.

To the reader: The fact that you hold this book, seemingly now at its conclusion, is as special a thanks as you can give to me. If anything I have written resonates or, better yet, activates action, then the efforts were all well spent.

Keep the faith, ever onward.